IMAGERY
Current Cognitive Approaches

CONTRIBUTORS

Theodore Xenophon Barber
B. R. Bugelski
Ralph Norman Haber
Allan Paivio
Sydney Joelson Segal

IMAGERY
Current Cognitive Approaches

Edited by Sydney Joelson Segal

CENTER FOR RESEARCH IN COGNITION AND AFFECT
CITY UNIVERSITY OF NEW YORK

ACADEMIC PRESS   New York and London   1971

ACADEMIC PRESS, INC.
111 Fifth Avenue, New York, New York 10003

United Kingdom Edition published by
ACADEMIC PRESS, INC. (LONDON) LTD.
24/28 Oval Road, London NW1 7DD

LIBRARY OF CONGRESS CATALOG CARD NUMBER: 71-159606

PRINTED IN THE UNITED STATES OF AMERICA

To my mother and my father

CONTENTS

LIST OF CONTRIBUTORS

Numbers in parentheses indicate the pages on which the authors' contributions begin.

Theodore Xenophon Barber (101), Medfield Foundation, Harding, Massachusetts

B. R. Bugelski (49), State University of New York at Buffalo, New York, New York

Ralph Norman Haber (33), Department of Psychology, University of Rochester, Rochester, New York

Allan Paivio (7), University of Western Ontario, London, Ontario

Sydney Joelson Segal (1, 69), Center for Research in Cognition and Affect, City University of New York, New York, New York

PREFACE

The recent revival of interest in internal processes, especially those generated by a conscious observer acting purposefully on his environment, has led psychologists to reconsider one of the oldest of mental phenomena: the internal picture or mental image. Holt commented on the revival of interest in imagery in 1964; but it has been especially in the last three or four years that systematic study of the image has engaged the attention of experimental psychologists (Hebb, 1968; Neisser, 1970; Bower, 1970; Richardson, 1969). Contemporary experimental approaches to the study of the image, however, are still relatively few, and there are only a handful of workers in the English-speaking world who have done extensive empirical research in this area.

The purpose of the conference on which this volume is based was to bring together five psychologists, each of whom had studied the image using an objective empirical approach. Each of these psychologists had an interest in imagery which predated the current burst of enthusiasm, and each approached the problem for somewhat idiosyncratic theoretical and empirical reasons. It is only in retrospect that the relevance of all these approaches to cognitive psychology is apparent, but it is this relevance which is the major reason for this publication.

The interested reader will find a summary of five different approaches to the study of the image, each internally consistent, although in many instances leading to views that diverge from one another. Although this is not a complete or exhaustive treatment, the scope is quite extensive, ranging from the brief image or icon, which serves as the source of storage in short-term memory, to global behavior changes, including hallucinatory imagery under the influence of drugs and hypnotic states. The role of the image in verbal learning and the relationship of the image to both sensory and cognitive aspects of perception are also considered. Empirical findings are quoted extensively, and each of the authors presents his own theoretical model, some obviously more complete than others. No attempt has been made to gloss over areas of controversy or disagreement; thus, the reader will notice certain disagreements in the conclusions of Segal and Barber, and — to a lesser extent — some disparities between Bugelski and Paivio. Despite the divergences in approach and conclusions, all the contributors adopt what is essentially a cognitive approach to imagery. The S-R reflex, which historically led to the extinction of interest in imagery, is eschewed in these papers. Instead, all essentially stress centralist positions, beginning with the conscious, purposeful observer, using many new techniques and sophisticated methodology to support that theoretical position.

Those who are interested in the broad area of cognitive psychology and who seek an introduction to current research in this area—graduate students, teachers, and researchers—will find this book of interest. It is likely that clinical psychologists and psychiatrists may also find this book of interest; as an adjunct to their current use of imagery as a technique in psychotherapy, they may wish to explore some of the empirical and theoretical aspects of imagery. Undoubtedly, the more serious student of cognitive psychology will use this as an introduction to further work of these five psychologists as well as to others whose works have been cited, whereas for the more casual student or the clinician, the book will provide an adequate summary of these writings.

The book opens with Allan Paivio's approach to imagery and language. Paivio's work is probably the best known in the area; he has done the most extensive research and has the most complete theoretical system. Some of the work described in his recent book is summarized. Haber has studied eidetic imagery in the past; he presents his analysis of the icon as an image and describes an ingenious series of recent experimental approaches to the measurement of this icon. Bugelski reports on a fairly recent series of experiments on imagery and evaluates the possibility of studying the image by empirical-behavioristic methods. Segal discusses a series of experiments which reveal important similarities between the processes of imaging and perceiving. Finally, Barber, whose work in the field of hypnotic research is well known, reviews his viewpoint and clearly indicates its relevance to the images and hallucinations which occur both under drug states and during hypnosis.

These papers were presented at a conference entitled "The Adaptive Function of Imagery," held June 5, 1970, at the Graduate Center of the City University of New York. The third conference in an annual series, it was sponsored by the Center for Research in Cognition and Affect. This Center was organized by Silvan Tomkins and Harold Proshansky, and is now under the directorship of Jerome L. Singer. The concern of Tomkins in imagery, of Proshansky in perception, and of Singer in daydreaming, mindwandering, and other fantasy experiences has long interested them in the problems of imagery and its measurement. I wish to express my gratitude especially to Harold Proshansky and Jerome Singer for their support of this conference. Other members of the Center also actively participated in this conference, and I want to thank William H. Ittelson, who served as chairman of the conference and gave valuable advice in planning the program, and also Charles Smith and Stanley Milgram for myriad acts of aid and encouragement. Finally, I wish to acknowledge my gratitude to Charles Segal, whose commitment to the furtherance of academic inquiry led him to render a generous gift from his family Foundation for the financial support of this conference.

SYDNEY JOELSON SEGAL

Bower, G. H. Analysis of a mnemonic device. *American Scientist,* 1970, **58**, 496-510.

Hebb, D. O. Concerning imagery. *Psychological Review,* 1968, **75**, 466-477.

Holt, R. R. Imagery: The return of the ostracized. *American Psychologist,* 1964, **12**, 254-264.

Neisser, U. Visual imagery as process and as experience. In J. S. Antrobus (Ed.), *Cognition and affect,* pp. 159-178. Little Brown: New York, 1970.

Richardson, A. *Mental imagery.* Springer: New York, 1969.

CHAPTER 1

INTRODUCTION

Sydney Joelson Segal

After forty years of studying man's behavior, psychologists are turning, some boldly, others surreptitiously, to the investigation of the human mind. The renewed interest in internal processes, gathering momentum over the past ten years, has been seized and defined by Ulric Neisser in his book on *Cognitive Psychology* (1967). When Neisser addressed the first conference of the City University's Center for Research in Cognition and Affect in June, 1967, imagery was the topic he chose. It was almost inevitable that the third conference of the center, seeking a contemporary topic in cognitive psychology, decided on current research in imagery. Since the conference of 1967 was held, there has been a steadily increasing amount of research relating to imagery. The contributors to this volume have all been active investigators of imagery long before the first conference was held, and all are able to report on consistent programs of research to support their viewpoints.

Describing imagery as a new or contemporary topic is strange, because the study of imagery has always been a part of the science of the mind; even during the dominance of Watson and behaviorism, imagery was studied by clinicians, and has crept into experimental literature under such pseudonyms as "conditioned hallucinations." Yet the very fact that imagery has always been with us as a part of our heritage derived from magic, religion, philosophy, and literature greatly complicates the problems faced by the investigator. It seems that we know so much about imagery, it is hard to recognize how little of what we know is documented, and how much of our knowledge is speculation. Imagery was recorded by Fechner, analyzed by Wundt, measured by Galton, discussed by

1

James, and introspectively dissected by Titchener. Any theoretical question one can postulate has already been reviewed exhaustively by philosophers, and many of the most ingenious experiments one can envisage have already been performed. The student of imagery tries to winnow out the empirical insights from the naive speculations that often accompany them.

There is a curious problem here, for it appears that many of the most naive beliefs came from the scientists themselves. Galileo, for example, ushered in the scientific age while asserting the primacy of the physical world and the unreliability of human sense impressions. Imagery, a sense impression without a corroborating physical attribute, was considered even less reliable than perception.

Even Galton, when he began to measure imagery with his famous breakfast table test, may have done the study of imagery something of a disservice. Galton emphasized the individual differences in vividness of imagery, and found that imagery was reported as more frequent and more vivid by children, housewives, and "common laborers," while it was less frequently reported and generally dimmer among "eminent men of science." This suggested to Galton that habits of abstract thought tend to reduce imagery. Thus, his conclusions were readily interpreted as signifying that imagery is the product of a relatively unsophisticated organism, and is not appropriately included among the higher cognitive functions.

At about this time, clinicians were describing delusions and hallucinations in a deranged spectrum of the population. Bleuler, for example, suggested a dichotomy in which vivid imaging seemed to be a defining characteristic of autism. Freud included imagery and hallucinations in the primary process functions related to drives, the more infantile needs, and wishes. Also, Levy-Bruhl observed the occurrence of animistic thinking in "primitive" cultures. Additionally, eidetic imagery was described in the 1920's, and was reported to have a more frequent rate of occurrence among children. All the reports seemed to follow true to type: imagery was an atavistic property of children, the primitive mentality, the regressed schizophrenic, still present in some "normal" adults, but virtually absent among those of higher intellect who concerned themselves with abstract thought.

In the early years of this century, while striving to build a psychology based on subjective conscious experiences, Titchener utilized introspection as the central tool and brought imagery to a position of great importance in his system. Though the psychophysicists found it difficult to measure imagery because there was no physical stimulus to correlate with the experience, for Titchener, on the other hand, imagery had a prominent role precisely because it did not depend on the stimulus. While Titchener seriously considered imagery as a basic cognitive function, there were certain flaws in this theory, and his study of imagery began to be hopelessly confounded with his introspective methods. Thus the study of imagery came to be avoided once more when the introspective techniques were replaced by Watson's behaviorism and Bridgman's operationism.

Recently, in trying to clarify the role of imagery as a cognitive function, Hebb found it necessary to indicate first how imagery could be studied without recourse to introspection. He questioned the entire concept of a mind turned in on itself, and indicated how imagery could be studied with the same objectivity as perception. He approached imagery as a cognitive function depending on some of the same cell assemblies and phase sequence units he had postulated for perception. Whether one agrees or disagrees with his physiology, it is part of the pragmatic approach to imagery that is now coming into prominence: imagery is there, it is a quality of human thinking, even of human behavior; how can it be measured?

Five chapters in this volume all approach this issue from different backgrounds, but with the common aim of finding how imagery functions, and how it can be measured and analyzed. There is a freedom in the use of methods which originated at many different times and places, but all of the methods are adapted to this purpose: to further the investigation and improve our understanding of imagery as a higher cognitive function.

Mnemonic devices, first studied by the Greek orators and practised over the years by mnemonists demonstrating their skill in night clubs, and by commercial memory schools, were resurrected by Miller, Galanter, and Pribram as an example of a highly productive and cohesive plan which served to organize data. In their paradigm, a subject first learned a mnemonic rhyme: "one is a bun, two is a shoe, three is a tree," etc., and then was given a list of ten words to learn. Subjects were allowed ample time between words, and were instructed to construct one image that included the bun and the first word, another image including the shoe and the second word, and so on. Miller *et al.* asserted that this technique should greatly facilitate learning and memory.

This mnemonic aid was studied experimentally both by Bugelski and by Paivio; both were able to confirm Miller *et al.*'s assertion, and both were able to extend the observation. Paivio had discovered that nouns seemed often to serve as conceptual pegs in paired-associate learning, just as the "bun" and the "shoe" did in Miller *et al.*'s rhyme, and he suggested that this might be due to image-arousing capabilities of nouns. In a succession of experiments, he systematically demonstrated that nouns, specifically concrete nouns, readily evoked mental imagery, and were easier to learn and recall than abstract or low-imagery nouns. In the course of this research, he developed norms to measure the image-arousing ability of words, as well as their concreteness, familiarity, and meaningfulness. Paivio used the norms as a basis for a factor-analysis of imagery; Bugelski also refers to the norms in Chapter 4 and discusses possible implications of the ratings, using them to suggest the outlines of a theoretical approach to meaning.

In Chapter 2, in developing the concept of two processing systems (the imagic and the verbal), Paivio discusses the role of imagery somewhat more specifically. He conceives imagery as a more primitive organizer than language, but is clearly aware of the reciprocity between the two. The relationship between imagery and language is also implicit in Chapter 3 by Ralph Haber. While the focus in his chapter is on the "visions" in perception, the icon which provides for short-term storage, he is concerned with the relationship of such icons to normal reading, and briefly refers to this point.

Haber, early in his career, was intrigued by the findings of Sperling, Averbach, and Coriell on short-term storage, and believed that parallels could be drawn to eidetic imagery. An eidetic image—like the icon—seemed to remain as an immediate aftereffect of retinal stimulation. Haber developed clear, simple, repeatable techniques for studying eidetic imagery, and was able to demonstrate many regularities of the phenomenon. However, his research left him with some of the same questions as the earlier investigators; he could not even obtain a correlation with the age of the subject, and was unable to relate the phenomenon to iconic storage.

At that point, he shifted back to his original interest in the icon, using some of the techniques he had developed in studying eidetic imagery and many new approaches to reveal more clearly how the nervous system possessed the capacity to prolong its awareness of a stimulus beyond the time when the stimulus had actually disappeared. Both eidetic imagery and its neighbor, the icon, are internal processes, which must be evaluated by ingenious use of verbal report techniques; and yet, because the eidetic image is present in a limited subset of the population and still seems something of a curiosity while the icon appears to be universal, the icon seemed more relevant to the study of imagery as a cognitive function.

Some of the constraints which were implicit in Haber's decision to shift from the study of eidetic imagery to the icon, thus moving from a somewhat phenomenological problem to a more universal cognitive process, are specifically spelled out in Bugelski's interesting chapter. Each of the writers in this book in some way comes to terms with the question of how imagery fits in with experimental psychology, and how experimental methods can be applied to imagery; Bugelski makes some of these questions explicit. Having watched the strange gyrations of the experimental psychological Zeitgeist over the past thirty years, he seems still amazed at the re-emergence of interest in such a subjective, mentalistic, inner experience as imagery.

Bugelski drew considerable attention to the study of imagery with his research on the mnemonic method of Miller *et al.*, and he has begun to investigate the importance of prior sensory experiences for imagery through the analysis of visual imagery in the congenitally blind and auditory imagery in the deaf. In his chapter he partly questions the justification for such research, and thereby raises issues which are of central concern to all workers in this field: the relationship of imagery to perception, on the one hand, to language and thought on the other; problems about how to analyze and measure imagery; and whether the same methods that apply to traditional issues in perception and learning can be effectively adapted to imaging. Chapter 4 does not present an integrated theoretical formulation, but the astute reader will find it to contain many ideas which can be further developed, many incipient approaches to problems in imagery which may be further explored.

The issues that Bugelski raises have almost been bypassed in the last two chapters. Both assume that these problems have been resolved, and exert considerable freedom in using hypothetical intervening constructs; both rely on past literature as well as on the authors' own research; and both attack issues which were an integral part of nineteenth century philosophical psychology.

My research (Chapter 5) was based on the classic study by Perky, a student in Titchener's laboratory, and consequently my report has reopened the philosophers' old question regarding the distinction between imagery and perception. Most research, even in the clinical field, assumes a clear distinction between these two processes; data questioning such an assumption have always been considered faintly mystical, even metaphysical. Thus, in resurrecting this issue and adopting some of the experiments and techniques of Titchener's laboratory, my chapter may expose itself to criticism on the grounds of naivete and sophistry.

Bugelski considered that the image differed from the perception because a stimulus was present during perception. I have used data from many antecedent experiments to indicate that a stimulus may also be present during imagery, so the image and percept are analogous, even overlapping processes. I have borrowed methods developed within contemporary psychophysics (chiefly signal detection methods and forced-choice procedures) to add objectivity to the verbal report and to give added empirical support to this hypothesis.

In Chapter 6, Barber raises some of the same questions. Hypnotism has always been treated gingerly by academic scientists; and even in the nineteenth century, scientists of the academies rejected the findings of Mesmer, Binet and Féré, and others. Barber has investigated the old findings and many of the old methods, but approaches the problem from such a contemporary viewpoint that the old objections no longer suffice. Many psychologists, in the nineteenth century and even today, approached hypnotism as a special or unique phenomenon, a mystical control of the mind, an altered state of consciousness.

In this book, Barber moves beyond the phenomenological approach to hypnotism. His real concerns seem to be the analysis and interpretation of verbal reports which describe imagery or hallucinatory experiences, and comparison of the reports obtained in a normal or control state, under hypnosis, and following ingestion of "hallucinogenic" drugs. If hypnotism really is an altered state of consciousness, then it should show similarities to drug effects; neatly and succinctly, he compares and contrasts effects reported under the two conditions. Both effects, in turn, are compared to effects reported by normal subjects; what was startling, even to Barber, was the frequency with which verbal reports of "hallucinations" were obtained in a normal, control population.

In the process of trying to measure imagery and of trying to distinguish the experiences of imagery from hallucinations, Barber has raised for us some basic questions concerning the validity of the verbal report, and the methods of approach to that report which may make it a more controlled and more useful dependent variable. Whereas most of the other investigators show the behaviorist's reluctance to rely fully on what the subject says, Barber has dealt more directly with subjective data.

While Barber's chapter shows more freedom in handling nonstimulus-bound concepts than any other in this book, the intent of it is clearly not anecdotal or phenomenological, but is a serious critical analysis of hallucinatory phenomena. In this way, it represents an experimental approach to the study of imagery, and is logically related to the intent of the volume. This point is especially clear when one recognizes the areas of research in imagery which were deliberately excluded from this book. Clinical research, imagery in children, cross-cultural research, study of schizophrenic hallucinations, and the current use of imagery techniques in psychotherapy, as well as many brilliant studies on individual differences in imaging, were all excluded. Barber's chapter has been used to represent the freest interpretation of imagery phenomena, as Haber's may depend least on the constructive or "imaginative" interpretation of imagery, and Bugelski's may represent the most conservative point of view.

Within the area defined by these viewpoints lies a range of experiences in which normal imagery has an important adaptive function; and that is the scope of this volume. Imagery is present in the iconic processing of sensory stimuli, in the integration of ambiguous stimuli into a cognitive experience, in differential interpretations of imagery in different states of consciousness, in the registration, coding, and storage of verbal materials, and in their retention and the ability to locate them for later recall. Imagery is a basic cognitive process, and it is not possible to study cognition adequately without elucidating the functions of imagery.

CHAPTER 2

IMAGERY AND LANGUAGE[1]

Allan Paivio

For a number of years my colleagues and I have been investigating the functions of imagery in learning, memory, and language. The work on learning and memory has been reviewed elsewhere recently (Paivio, 1969, 1970), as has related research by others (e.g., Bower, 1970; Reese, 1970; Rohwer, 1970). Therefore, a discussion of the general background is unnecessary here, and I will deal primarily with those aspects of the program that have been concerned with language, especially at the level of phrases and sentences. First, I will discuss the theoretical and empirical views that have guided the research, then I will review some specific evidence pertaining to the psycholinguistic problems of meaning, comprehension, and the learning and retention of verbal material.

The major theoretical assumption here is that language is closely linked to two basic coding systems, or cognitive modes. One mode is related directly to speech itself; that is, we can think in terms of words and their interrelations and these implicit verbal processes can mediate our language behavior. The other code is nonverbal and is presumably tied closely to the private experience that we call imagery. Thus, if I say to you, "The red-haired boy is peeling a green orange," your comprehension of the phrase is likely to include some kind of mental picture of the boy and the orange, together with implicit activities related to peeling oranges, not

[1] Much of the research described in this report was supported by research grants from the National Research Council of Canada (Grant APA-87) and the University of Western Ontario Research Fund.

merely silent rehearsal of the words themselves. The language code has flipped over into a nonverbal one and, if I now ask you to remember the sentence, you might do so by remembering the objects and actions involved in the image and then reconstructing the sentence from them. Since the sentence input and the output are verbal, some rapid transformations to the nonverbal code and back again to the verbal one must occur if this assumption is correct. This means that the two systems are interconnected and that it is possible to get from one to the other very easily.

The view that the comprehension and production of language can be mediated by nonverbal imagery seems perfectly reasonable at a commonsense level, but the notion has been repeatedly opposed in psychology. The grounds for the negative attitude have been summarized by Roger Brown (1958) in his critique of the imagery interpretation of meaning, that is, the idea that the "click of comprehension" of a word is the occurrence of an image when the word is heard. One argument, aired by various writers from Bishop Berkeley on, is that words—even specific words like "dog"—are generic or abstract in meaning whereas images are specific. Other arguments refer to the apparent lack of empirical support for the image theory: some people lack imagery, or the images they report are too variable to be an appropriate basis for explaining reference. Still another argument is that images are aroused too slowly to be useful as mediators of language behavior. The last point has been expressed most recently by Wickens and Engle (1970) in a paper on imagery in short-term memory.

I have discussed these issues at length elsewhere (Paivio, 1971) and will only touch on them here. The main counterarguments are as follows: (a) images may be schematic rather than highly specific forms of representation; (b) they need not be consciously reportable to be functional—a point expressed in different terms by Neisser (1968) in a paper presented at the Annual Conference of the Center for Research in Cognition and Affect; (c) *meaning,* from a psychological viewpoint, need not be fixed but may vary from time to time, depending on the set created by prior events and the situational context of the moment; and (d) images can arise more quickly as a reaction to stimuli than has been supposed. Finally, it is important to note that I am not suggesting that meaning *is* an image—the term, meaning, has broader significance than that. What I am claiming is that imagery can and does occur as an associative reaction to words, and that it plays a part in our memory for (and comprehension of) language. I will rely primarily on experimental evidence and the reader can judge for himself whether the concept of imagery has utility in relation to the psychology of language. First, I will present a more detailed overview of the conceptual and empirical approach we have followed.

THE PRESENT APPROACH

We have generally assumed that imagery cannot be understood in isolation but only in comparison or contrast with other constructs, among which verbal thought is of paramount importance. Thus we have attempted to distinguish imaginal and verbal processes theoretically and empirically. Theoretically, the lines are drawn in terms of functional distinctions between the symbolic systems. Two of these postulated distinctions are relevant here. According to one of these, imagery is specialized for the symbolic representation of *concrete* situations and events, whereas the verbal system is characterized by its capacity to deal with more *abstract* stimulus information. The second distinction contrasts *parallel* and *sequential* information processing. Visual imagery, like visual perception, is assumed to be a parallel-processing system in the visual-spatial sense. Units of information are stored as visual entities, and any organization into higher order units is spatial rather than sequential in nature. The verbal system, on the other hand, is specialized for processing information sequentially. The implications of these functional distinctions should become clear in the context of relevant research, to be discussed presently.

In regard to the empirical approach, we have defined and distinguished imagery from verbal processing in terms of three classes of operations, including (a) measures of stimulus meaning, particularly its abstractness-concreteness or image-arousing value; (b) experimental manipulations, such as instructions designed to prime (or increase) the availability of imagery; and (c) individual differences in imaginal or verbal symbolic habits or skills. Since most of the research evidence centers around the meaning definition, a more detailed theoretical analysis and some preliminary research evidence bearing on that approach will be discussed next.

IMAGERY AND MEANING

I believe that, as psychologists, we have no alternative but to view meaning in terms of the covert and overt reactions that are elicited by nonverbal objects, words, and other signs. Of course, as Roger Brown (1958) has insisted, such reactions need not always be manifested in any measurable form and it is therefore appropriate to think of meaning as a response *disposition,* provided that we clearly recognize that the nature of such meaning dispositions cannot be understood except through their behavioral manifestations. When we speak of word meaning, therefore, we are referring to the relevance of the word as a stimulus for the *activation* of a correlated disposition within the person. Meaning reactions are the *aroused,* covert (that is, inferred) or overt expressions of the organismic dispositions. It is not necessary for our purposes to speculate about the nature of the organismic dispositions, although an analysis such as Hebb's (1949), in terms of cell assemblies and phase sequences capable of forming new associations (that is, new meanings) and having connections with various afferent and motor systems, would be an acceptable kind of approach. In agreement with theorists such as Osgood (1953), Werner and Kaplan (1963), and others, I assume that the aroused meaning process evoked by a word or other symbol is an organismic reaction with affective, or motor (including verbal), or imaginal components, or all of these at once. The reaction may be unconscious, not verbalizable, or it may be short-circuited, in either case resulting in behaviors not preceded by reportable mental content, including imagery. Moreover, I explicitly assume that the meaning reaction aroused by a stimulus is variable, as Titchener insisted long ago. That is, the particular meaning reaction to a stimulus is not fixed but will vary from time to time depending on the set created by prior events and the situational context of the moment. Nevertheless, some reactions to a particular symbol are more consistent than others and it is these which define the dominant psychological meaning of the concept.

These organismic reactions that are the psychological basis of stimulus meaning can be regarded as a series of transformations and elaborations of the incoming stimulus information. While not always related explicitly to the concept of meaning, such an approach to information transmission within the individual is generally accepted in contemporary psychology. Various terms such as coding, mediation, and information processing have been used to label the relevant processes, and numerous theoretical models are based on some kind of hierarchical elaboration of the properties of such concepts. Representative of such models are contemporary approaches to perception and memory, in which the postulated processes range from a short-duration perceptual image of the stimulus input, through short-term, to long-term memory systems with various theoretical properties (see Atkinson and Shiffrin, 1968; Neisser, 1967). The theoretical analysis I have proposed involves a specific interpretation of the nature of the coding processes involved at different levels of the processing of stimulus information. The levels might be continuous, but it simplifies matters to postulate 4 discrete levels. The first level is the rapidly fading perceptual image or "iconic" memory, proposed by Sperling (1960), or its acoustic analog, as identified by Crowder and Morton (1969), which refers to relatively untransformed information that is retained for a brief period following stimulus exposure. Such a perceptual trace can be viewed as a zero-point in a scale of meaning reactions, since the properties of the transient trace presumably are unaffected by operations that define higher order meaning (cf. Haber's review of the visual storage system in this book, Chapter 3). All further levels, however, do involve processes that are theoretically and operationally linked to meaning. I have referred to these as *representational, referential,* and *associative* levels of meaning. Each level involves either imaginal or verbal symbolic processes, or both, and the analysis applies to nonverbal as well as to verbal stimuli, although our concern here is only with verbal stimuli.

The representational level refers to hypothetical symbolic representations that are stored in long-term memory as concrete images in the case of stimulus objects, and as implicit auditory-motor representations in the case of verbal stimuli. At this level, objects and words as stimuli activate the corresponding representational processes within the individual. Such a representational process can be regarded as corresponding to Hebb's cell assembly, which he defines as "the simplest instance of a representative process (image or idea) (1949, p. 60)." In the case of verbal representations, the process corresponds rather directly to Bousfield's (1961) concept of the representational response, which refers to the implicit or explicit emission of the word itself as the initial reaction to a verbal stimulus. This level of meaning corresponds intuitively to familiarity in the most elementary sense of "knowing" the stimulus. Familiarity implies that some organismic representation of a stimulus is "available." Further associative connections may be lacking, however, in which case the stimulus has no higher order (referential or associative) meaning.[2]

The second level, referential meaning, assumes associative connections between imaginal and verbal representations, such that an object or picture can be named, and the name can evoke an image. The reactions in each case are referential or denotative in nature. The third level, associative meaning, refers to sequences or patterns of associations involving words, images, or both. It includes associative meaning in the traditional sense of intraverbal associations and in addition incorporates the assumption of imaginal associative chains or structures.

It can be seen that the three postulated levels of meaning vary according to the degree to which a given verbal or nonverbal stimulus is, in Bartlett's terms, "connected with something else (Bartlett, 1932, pp. 44–45)."

Various defining operations can be specified for each level, but I have assumed that latency measures or their analogs are the most appropriate indices of the availability of the underlying processes. Representational meaning would accordingly be indexed by the speed of perceptual recognition as reflected in reaction time measures; duration thresholds, familiarity ratings, and frequency counts would be appropriate correlates. Referential meaning would be measured by latency of labeling an object, or the latency of image arousal to words or

---

[2] This use of the term "representational process" is to be distinguished from Osgood's concept of the "representational mediation process," which refers to a higher level of meaning than is intended here.

sentences; ratings of ease of imagery or concreteness are correlated analogs of image latency. Associative meaning should be similarly indexed by measures of associative latency.

RELATION BETWEEN STIMULUS ABSTRACTNESS-CONCRETENESS AND THE LEVELS-OF-MEANING ANALYSIS

Given the preceding theoretical groundwork, we can now consider the stimulus dimension which is most relevant to the balance of the chapter, namely abstractness-concreteness. The major assertion is that *concrete and abstract language differ primarily in referential meaning:* concrete words or passages readily evoke images of the objects and events to which the concrete language refers, whereas abstract words or passages do not evoke images so readily. Note that this is a relative distinction, inasmuch as it does not imply that abstract language can *not* arouse imagery, only that it does so less readily than concrete (cf. Bugelski's discussion of the same issue in Chapter 4 of this book). Concrete and abstract language, however, need not differ in representational meaning (familiarity), nor in their capacity to arouse other words as associative reactions.

EXPERIMENTAL EVIDENCE

Our attempts to validate the preceding view of concrete and abstract meaning have invariably involved comparisons of different levels or different kinds of meaning. In one study this was done by means of a factor analysis of word attributes (Paivio, 1968). Forty-eight concrete and 48 abstract nouns were selected as the "subjects" and group data on various attributes were obtained using rating scale, association, and other methods. The crucial questions were: which attributes will covary with concreteness, and which will be the best predictors of criterial performance measures of learning and memory? The study yielded 6 factors, of which the strongest was an imagery-concreteness factor defined by a reaction time measure of image latency and rating-scale measures of concreteness, tangibility, ease of image arousal, and vividness of imagery. This factor also was easily the best predictor of the ease of learning and remembering the items. Frequency and familiarity measures defined another factor, indicating that criterial measures of representational meaning (as specified by the meaning theory) are independent of imaginal referential meaning. Numerous other relations from the analysis are interesting, but only indirectly relevant to the present discussion.

Other evidence comes from reaction time studies which sought to distinguish between imagery and other meaning reactions. A recent, unpublished experiment by Simpson (1970) at Carleton University compared imagery and representation reaction times to noun stimuli that varied in familiarity, or in rated concreteness and imagery according to our published norms for 925 nouns (Paivio, Yuille, and Madigan, 1968). The findings are relevant to the distinction between levels of meaning as well as to the important question of whether imagery can occur quickly enough to verbal stimuli to be of any functional significance in mediating comprehension or other language phenomena.

Representational reaction time was defined as the time required to recognize a word. Referential imagery was defined as the latency of image arousal to the word. Subjects in each condition were carefully instructed on what was meant by recognition or imagery, and reaction time was measured by a key press. Simpson predicted that recognition speed would vary with word familiarity but not with word imagery. Figure 1A shows the results which confirmed the predictions. Referential imagery, on the other hand, was expected to vary with the word's imagery-concreteness level but not with its familiarity. The confirmatory results are shown in Fig. 1B.

Simpson replicated part of the study in a further experiment which involved 2 additional variables. One was repeated trials to assess the effect of practice; the other variable involved the use of the same list as compared to different lists of words on each trial. Simpson expected that practice *with the same words* would result in faster reactions over repeated trials. In the imagery condition, this was expected to occur particularly when the words are abstract. The subjects

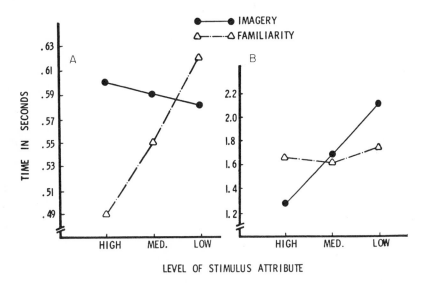

Fig. 1. Reaction time for word recognition (A) and imagery (B) responses as a function of rated imagery-concreteness and familiarity. (Reproduced with the permission of H. M. Simpson, Carleton University, Canada.)

presumably would have difficulty discovering an image to such words initially, but they may remember their previous imaginal associations and react increasing quickly over trials.

The results for the recognition response measure are shown in Fig. 2. The only significant effect was that of repeated trials, indicating that subjects benefited slightly from practice. As in the first experiment, high imagery and low imagery words did not differ in recognition speed. The contrasting results for imagery reaction time are shown in Fig. 3. It can be seen that, even after 4 trials, imagery occurred more slowly to low imagery than to high imagery words. In addition to validating the rating measure of imagery, this finding is important because it indicates that the difference in imagery latency is stable and reliable, not eliminated by practice on the image-generation task. The triple interaction also was significant, indicating, as predicted, that the latency reduction over trials occurred primarily when the same low imagery words were repeated. When different words were presented on each trial, there was an inexplicable reduction in reaction time on trial 2, but a return to the first trial baseline on subsequent trials.

The other important point to note in regard to these findings is the absolute latency of imagery. Values of the order of 1.5 seconds for image arousal to concrete words were reported by Moore (1915), and we have obtained longer latencies in our studies (e.g., Paivio, 1966). As noted earlier, this has been taken as evidence that imagery occurs too slowly to play any functional role in language behavior (e.g., Wickens and Engle, 1970). Note, however, that the reaction time is *not* representative of the latency of the *mental event* called imagery, since the RT includes simple motor RT and whatever decision processes are involved in the experimental task. Simpson succeeded in reducing some of this "excess baggage" by careful instructions and the use of preliminary practice trials so that the "raw" image RT to high imagery (concrete) words in his second experiment was around .9–1.0 seconds

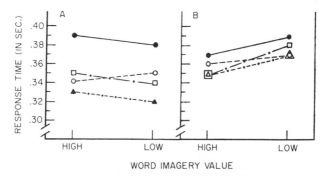

Fig. 2. Recognition response time as a function of word imagery level and trials when the same word list (A) or different lists (B) are used on 4 different trials: 1, closed circle; 2, open circle; 3, open square; and 4, closed triangle. (Reproduced with the permission of H. M. Simpson, Carleton University, Canada.)

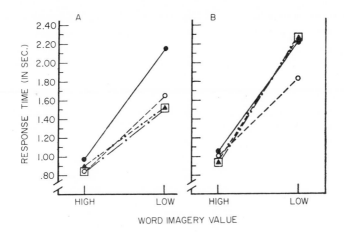

Fig. 3. Imagery response time as a function of word imagery level and trials, with the same list (A) or different lists (B) of words over 4 trials: 1, closed circle; 2, open circle; 3, open square; and 4, closed triangle. (Reproduced with the permission of H. M. Simpson, Carleton University, Canada.)

on the average. Using Donders' method and subtracting recognition response time from image RT, we are left with a value of around .6 seconds for the arousal of imagery. Comparable values for the generation of "visual information" have been reported by Posner, Boies, Eichelman, and Taylor (1969; also see Tversky, 1969). It is probably safe to conclude that imagery can be aroused by concrete verbal material within ½ second or so after the word has been read—fast enough to play a mediational function in many instances of language behavior. Moreover, imagery might be primed by contextual cues and occur even more quickly in natural language situations than in the laboratory tasks under consideration here.

The next study to be discussed involved a comparison of imagery and verbal associative RT, along with individual differences in imagery ability. Carole Ernest and I have investigated individual differences in a series of studies, using spatial manipulation tests and imagery questionnaires to categorize subjects as high or low in imagery ability (e.g., Ernest and Paivio, 1969). The study to be considered here (Ernest and Paivio, 1971) involved imagery ability, concrete and abstract stimulus words, and instructional sets, and required that a key be pressed either when an image occurred or when a verbal associate was aroused. We expected that verbal associative RT would not differ for concrete and abstract words, whereas the usual imagery difference should occur. The confirming interaction is shown in Fig. 4, which replicates similar results from an earlier experiment (Paivio, 1966).

We also expected an interaction involving imagery ability. Since the meaning of concrete words is assumed to be tied closely to imagery, both groups should readily experience images to such stimuli, but the superior imagery ability of high

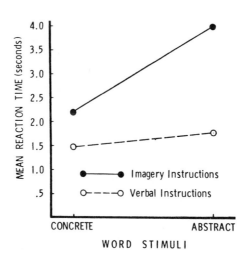

Fig. 4. Imagery and verbal associative reaction time for concrete and abstract nouns.

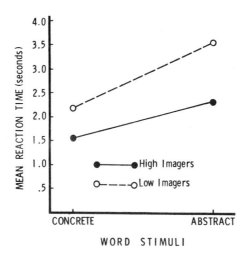

Fig. 5. Mean reaction time of high and low imagery subjects to concrete and abstract stimulus words.

imagers should show up when the words are abstract. The results were in the appropriate direction but the required triple interaction was not significant. Instead, we obtained the significant double interaction of concreteness and imagery ability shown in Fig. 5. High imagery subjects reacted more quickly than low imagers under *both* the imaginal and the verbal associative sets, and this difference was particularly great when the stimulus words were abstract. Several interpretations are possible, but the one we favor is that verbal associations, too, can be mediated by imagery. This is supported by the factor analytic study described earlier (Paivio, 1968) in which verbal associative meaningfulness *(m)* loaded substantially on the imagery-concreteness factor. The data in that study also showed that *m* correlated more highly with *imaginal* reaction time than with verbal associative RT, indicating that the number of associations a word evokes is related more closely to the speed with which images are aroused than to the speed of verbal reactions. The individual differences study similarly showed that, while imagery ability predicted imaginal and verbal latencies, measures of *verbal* symbolic habits obtained in the same study were uncorrelated with the reaction time data. The generalization from these findings is that the speed of higher order meaning reactions to verbal stimuli is more closely related to variables that define imagery processes than they are to those that define verbal processes.

To summarize, the reaction time data show that imagery reaction time is a function of word concreteness, but not of word familiarity and, conversely, that word recognition time is related to familiarity but not to concreteness. The latter finding is also consistent with perceptual threshold data: Paivio and O'Neill (1970) showed recently that tachistoscopic thresholds are unrelated to imagery and concreteness, but word familiarity, as usual, was highly effective. These findings indicate that immediate perceptual recognition does not require the arousal of higher order meaning reactions such as imagery, but imagery can occur reasonably quickly as an associative reaction, particularly when the words are concrete. It remains to be demonstrated now that such imagery can be functional in language behavior.

IMAGERY AND LANGUAGE COMPREHENSION

The following series of studies extend the analysis to the relations between imagery and comprehension, using sentences rather than individual words as stimuli. Imagery was assumed to be functionally related to comprehension, particularly in the case of concrete language. Bugelski (1969) has recently presented such a theoretical approach in regard to reading for meaning, and Huttenlocher (1968) has interpreted syllogistic reasoning in terms of spatial imagery aroused by the language in which a problem is stated. Our approach to the issue has involved comparisons of comprehension and imagery latencies.

Ian Begg and I (Paivio and Begg, 1970) reasoned that if imagery contributes to reading comprehension then comprehension and image latencies should be substantially correlated. Indeed, imagery should precede understanding in time, although this expectation was not supported by Moore's (1915) early research on meaning and imagery reaction times, which showed that meaning generally preceded imagery. Moore's finding is not damaging to the imagery position, since, as noted earlier, it is not necessary to assume that images are consciously experienced in order for them to be effective, any more than associationistic approaches or theories based on transformational grammar call for conscious correlates of associative habits or transformational rules. Nevertheless, in view of Moore's results, we did not expect to find imagery preceding comprehension in our laboratory tests. Instead, we expected strong correlations between the two kinds of reactions, and interactions between the concreteness level of the stimulus material and the conditions designed to arouse imagery and comprehension.

One of 2 experiments involved presentations of a series of typed sentences of various syntactical types under 1 of 4 instructional sets: reading, imaging, comprehending, or paraphrasing. A sentence was exposed and the subject pressed a key when he had completed the required task. Correlations were computed between the mean latencies for individual sentences under each instructional set—that is, the sentences were the "subjects." Imagery, comprehension, and paraphrasing were all highly correlated (.76 to .83). The correlations between reading and the other tasks were lower, ranging from .44 to .66. With reading latency partialed out, imagery, comprehension, and paraphrasing remained highly correlated, ranging from .69 to .77.

The correlational data suggest a common process, but they provided no basis for any particular causal interpretation. Unexpectedly, however, the mean latencies showed an orderly progression for all sentence types with reading being fastest, followed by imagery, then by comprehension, and finally by paraphrasing. The surprising result was that imagery was slightly, but consistently, *faster* than comprehension or paraphrasing. Considered together, the correlations and mean differences in latencies suggest that imagery makes it easier to understand and to paraphrase sentences. The faster latency for imagery than for comprehension is directly contrary to the earlier data on imagery and meaning, but the latter research was concerned only with individual words, and the reversal may have occurred because of the greater complexity of sentences. It is possible, for example, that subjects generated images only to part of a sentence, whereas comprehension required processing of the entire string of words.

A second experiment investigated image and comprehension latencies using both abstract and concrete sentences. It involved 50 concrete and 50 abstract sentences taken from an earlier memory experiment by Begg and Paivio (1969) which I will describe later. An example of a sentence categorized as being relatively concrete is *The spirited leader slapped a mournful hostage.* An example of an abstract sentence is *The arbitrary regulation provoked a civil complaint.* The sentences were presented one at a time using a tachistoscope. The subject pressed a button to expose the sentence, and released it as soon as he had an image or understood the sentence.

On the basis of the kind of reasoning that I have been discussing here, as well as previous empirical findings, we expected an interaction between concreteness and the image-versus-comprehension instructional variable. The meaning of abstract sentences, like that of abstract nouns or noun pairs, is presumably tied more closely to the intraverbal context and verbal associative reactions than to imagery. Abstract sentences, therefore, should arouse images only with difficulty and yet be understandable on the basis of their intraverbal meaning. This distinction should be reflected in much longer latencies for imagery than for comprehension. On the other hand, the meaning of concrete sentences is closely tied to concrete referents and their imaginal representations; this close relationship should be reflected in relatively small differences between image and comprehension latencies. Figure 6 shows a significant interaction entirely in accord with our predictions. Subjects required much more time to generate images to abstract sentences than to understand them. The difference was in the same direction, but was much smaller for concrete sentences. Moreover, image latencies were longer for abstract than for concrete sentences, but comprehension latencies did not differ significantly for the two kinds of material. The interaction indicates that imagery and comprehension cannot be equated, but it also suggests that they are much more closely related when the material is concrete than when it is abstract. This was confirmed by a correlational analysis involving mean comprehension and imagery latencies for each sentence, as in the first experiment. The correlation between comprehension and imagery was .71 for concrete sentences and significantly lower, .60, for

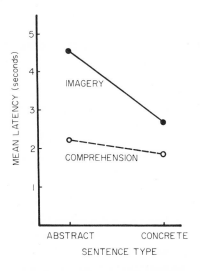

Fig. 6. Imagery and comprehension latencies for abstract and concrete sentences.

abstract sentences. Nevertheless, when concrete and abstract sentences were pooled, the correlation was .83, exactly the same as the value obtained in the first experiment.

The reversal in the direction of the difference between imagery and comprehension latencies for concrete sentences in the two experiments presumably resulted from some systematic difference in the structure of the sentences involved, but the problem remains to be resolved at this time. The general conclusion is that imagery and comprehension are closely related processes, particularly in the case of concrete sentences, where imagery and comprehension can occur at comparable speeds. Research based on this approach is only beginning, but the theoretical viewpoint and the findings to date have implications for the psycholinguistic literature on comprehension, particularly in view of the fact that highly concrete, picturable material has been used almost invariably in such research. The relevance of imagery is particularly apparent in studies in which subjects are required to verify the truth or falsity of a sentence against a picture depicting events that may or may not correspond to those suggested by a stimulus sentence (e.g., Gough, 1965). Such matters have been discussed at length elsewhere (Paivio, 1971).

IMAGERY AND MEMORY FOR CONNECTED DISCOURSE

We turn next to the function of imagery in memory for language. Numerous studies (see Paivio, 1969) have established clearly that the image-arousing value of words is the most potent variable yet identified among meaningful material in learning and memory tasks. For example, high imagery words are superior to low in free recall, recognition memory, verbal discrimination learning, and (especially) paired-associate learning. In the case of paired-associate learning, the positive effect of imagery is greater when varied among stimulus members than when varied among response members of the pairs. I have interpreted this result to mean that imagery is particularly important in the retrieval phase of the task. These effects have been obtained most often when using familiar nouns, but they have also been obtained with adjectives (e.g., Yuille, Paivio, and Lambert, 1969). A recent experiment by Philipchalk and Begg (1970) shows the comparable effects of adjective and noun imagery. The study included a comparison of several learning tasks, but a description of the paired-associate learning experiment will suffice for present purposes. The to-be-learned items included high and low imagery nouns, and adjectives associated with nonsense syllables embedded in sentence fragments. Thus one list contained such items as "The QOF blister," another "The rusty QOF," a third "The QOF explanation," and a fourth "The basic QOF"; here *blister* and *rusty* are relatively concrete, whereas *explanation* and *basic* are relatively abstract.

A study-test procedure was used in such a way that the sentence fragments were first shown successively, then the sentence frames were presented with the nonsense syllables missing and the subject attempted to fill in the blanks. Thus the nouns and adjectives, in effect, functioned as stimuli for the recall of the associated syllable. The results for 4 trials are presented in Fig. 7, where it can be seen that concreteness (i.e., high imagery) for both nouns and adjectives strongly facilitated associative recall. Moreover, the effects of noun imagery and adjective imagery were approximately equal, as evidenced by the fact that the interaction of form class and concreteness was not significant. Nouns on the average were somewhat better cues than adjectives, although this effect also failed to reach significance. The results suggest that stimulus imagery has a strong effect on associative recall whether varied within nouns or adjectives, provided that the range of imagery variation is comparable in the 2 classes.

I will now consider in more detail the implications of imagery and the dual-coding model generally for memory for connected discourse, that is, for phrases, sentences, and paragraphs. Let us begin with a reminder of the theoretical position. Extended to connected discourse, the dual process model implies that concrete phrases or sentences, like concrete words, can be coded and stored in memory, not only verbally, but also in the form of nonverbal imagery. In the case of concrete sentences, such as *The boy hit the girl,* imagery predominates. In the case of abstract material such as *The theory has predictive value,* the message is more likely to be stored only in its verbal form. The analysis has interesting implications regarding memory for connected verbal material. Note especially that, although high imagery words or paired associates are generally easier to learn and

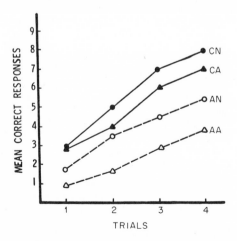

Fig. 7. Associative recall of nonsense syllables over trials when the stimulus members were concrete nouns (CN), abstract nouns (AN), concrete adjectives (CA), or abstract adjectives (AA). [Data from Philipchalk and Begg (1970).]

remember than low imagery ones, the model does not imply that high imagery *sentences* will necessarily be remembered better than low imagery sentences. If concrete material indeed tends to be coded in a nonverbal form, then it must be decoded back in order to generate the correct verbal output. Decoding errors are therefore possible, especially in regard to such features of language as its grammatical form and precise wording. Of course, this is not really incompatible with the expectations and findings regarding individual words or word pairs. Decoding errors are also possible in connection with imagery mediation of paired-associate learning, or the recall of individual items, but the negative effect is presumably minimal where the words have relatively specific, readily named referents. The appropriate generalization is that imagery may either facilitate or hinder memory for language, depending on such factors as the length of the to-be-remembered verbal units and which features of the message are to be recalled. Imagery may enable one to retrieve the general theme of the message and perhaps even some of its word units, but not necessarily its grammatical form.

One experimental implication of the dual-coding model was tested in a situation involving memory for connected discourse. Lachman and his associates at The University of New York in Buffalo (e.g., Pompi and Lachman, 1967) proposed that memory for connected discourse is in the form of surrogate structures or processes, where surrogate process refers to a general idea, theme, or image. Such a process is what is stored in memory, and the wording itself is reconstructed from the general idea during recall of the passage. In support of this view, these investigators obtained somewhat better recall for passages that were presented in a thematically organized manner than for the same passages presented in random order, even when the subjects were not required to recall thematically, but only needed to produce individual words. Moreover, theme-related errors were more frequent in the case of the thematically presented passages.

Yuille and I (Yuille and Paivio, 1969) extended the Lachman-type study by varying concreteness of the passage in addition to its degree of thematic organization. We expected that thematic organization during input would have a greater facilitating effect in the case of concrete passages than in the case of abstract, because the concrete material can be coded in the form of images. The experiment required the subjects to recall words from 1 of 3 passages—1 highly concrete passage, 1 that was of medium concreteness, or 1 that was highly abstract. The material was presented for 2 study and recall trials, in either a syntactically organized or in a random order. The results are shown in Fig. 8, where it can be seen that on the second trial recall of concrete material was facilitated by thematic order, but no such effect occurred in the case of medium or highly abstract passages. Although other interpretations are possible, these findings are consistent with the idea that thematic presentation in the case of highly concrete passages permits the subject to generate a visual image of the setting of the story together with some of the salient elements in it, and from such an organized, thematic image

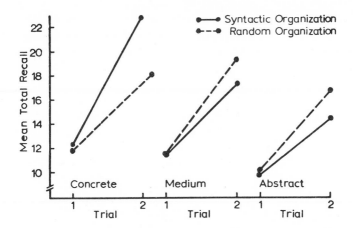

Fig. 8. Mean total recall scores for each trial as a function of abstractness and level of organization of the passage. [Based on data from Yuille and Paivio (1969).]

to reconstruct the verbal content. This is conceptually related to the effect of stimulus imagery in paired-associate learning in that the image in the present case also provided an effective means of retrieving associated information that had previously been presented in the connected passage (or so we assumed). The general implication is that even thematic organization does not facilitate memory for highly abstract material, at least only in a trial or two. The facilitating effect in the case of concrete material occurred presumably because the subject was required to recall only words and not syntactical order.

This leads us to research concerned with memory for meaning, as compared to memory for the wording of sentences. Studies by Jacqueline Sachs (1967a, b) formed the point of departure for the research. The subjects in her experiment listened to recorded passages of connected discourse and, immediately after each passage, one of the sentences from it was repeated. The repeated test sentence was either identical to one in the passage or it was changed in some slight way and the subjects were asked to state whether it was "changed" or "identical." When changes occurred, they were either semantic, syntactical, or lexical. The semantic changes were achieved by interchanging the subject and the object in the sentence or phrase, by negation, or by substitution of a word that occurred elsewhere in the passage. For example, the sentence "The boy hit the girl" might be played back as "The girl hit the boy." Syntactical and lexical changes involved changes in wording which did not alter the meaning of the sentence; for example, a change from active to passive voice or vice versa, or by the substitution of a synonym. Thus *The boy hit the girl* might be played back as *The girl was hit by the boy,* or *The lad hit the girl.* Sachs found that if the test sentence was played back immediately after the original sentence the accuracy of the judgments of identity and change was high for all test sentences. However, if some additional verbal material was interpolated between the original sentence and the playback of it, recognition for the syntactic changes or the wording of the sentence dropped sharply to a near chance level while the recognition of semantic changes remained high. Sachs concluded that the original form of the sentence is stored only for the short time necessary for comprehension to occur. Thereafter, the specific wording fades rapidly from memory. When a semantic interpretation has been made the meaning is stored and memory for the meaning is not dependent on memory of the original form of the sentence. Later recall of the sentence is a reconstruction from the remembered meaning rather than a verbatim recall. Essentially the same view has been expressed by Bregman and Strasberg (1968).

Sach's conclusions are essentially correct for certain types of material, but they need to be qualified. Begg and Paivio (1969) recently tested the implications, for the Sachs phenomenon, of the two-process model under consideration here. Let me rephrase the main point. A concrete sentence such as "The fat boy kicked a girl" can be imaginally represented as an action picture in which the meaning of the entire sentence is summarized as a single organized unit or complex image. On the other hand, the information contained in abstract material, such as "The theory has predictive power," remains more closely linked to the sequentially organized verbal units themselves and can be summarized as an imaginal unit only with difficulty, if at all. It follows that the most effectively coded, stored, and retrieved aspects of a concrete sentence will be those related to the sentence as a whole unit, such as its meaning. In abstract sentences, however, the specific words will be relatively better remembered. The material used by Sachs was relatively concrete and her results are consistent with the hypothesis as it pertains to such sentences. The converse prediction for abstract material was not tested by Sachs.

Begg and I evaluated the hypothesis using essentially the same design as Sachs, with the addition that relatively abstract as well as concrete sentences were included in the design. The subjects heard a series of sentences, then one of these was played back either in its original form or changed semantically or in wording. Our specific expectations were that semantic changes would be recognized better than changes in wording that do not affect meaning in the case of concrete material. This would replicate the Sachs finding. Conversely, changes in wording should be better recognized than changes in meaning in the case of abstract material. The results are shown in Fig. 9, which shows a striking interaction that precisely confirmed both predictions. These results suggest that concrete meaning, once aroused, is not dependent on the words themselves, but is stored in a nonverbal code and, indeed, the words can be forgotten while their nonverbal meaning is retained. The meaning of abstract material, however, is tied to the wording itself, and to remember the meaning is to remember the specific wording.

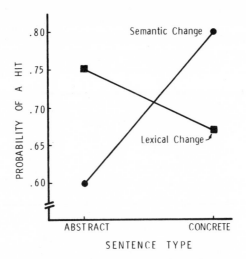

Fig. 9. Correct recognition of semantic and lexical changes as a function of the abstractness-concreteness of sentences. [From Begg and Paivio (1969).]

IMAGERY VERSUS DEEP STRUCTURE IN MEMORY

The next study concerns an alternative interpretation of the kinds of psycholinguistic findings that I have attributed to imagery. Earlier I noted that word imagery was a better predictor of the memorability and associative learning of words than a large number of other semantic or meaning attributes. In the immediately preceding studies, however, we were dealing, not with single words, but with phrases, sentences, or passages. Perhaps the findings could be explained better in terms of a recent approach based on contemporary linguistic theory than in terms of imagery.

The reference here is to the theory of transformational generative grammar as formulated by Chomsky (1965), which has persuaded many psychologists to abandon their traditional approaches to the psychology of language. One of the important features of Chomsky's approach is the distinction between the surface structure and the deep structure of a sentence, which corresponds roughly to the commonsense distinction between the actual wording of a sentence and its underlying meaning. For example, we readily understand that the sentence, *The boy is hitting the girl,* has essentially the same meaning as *The girl is being hit by the boy,* although the two sentences differ in their superficial grammatical structure. Chomsky's analysis specifies this essential similarity by showing that both sentences have a common underlying structure. More generally, the model indicates how various syntactic forms such as passives, negatives, and questions represent transformations of more elementary or basic linguistic structures, which are operated upon by certain transformational rules to yield the surface sentences.

A number of psycholinguists have based their theories of comprehension and memory for sentences on this general model. For example, George Miller (1962) at one time suggested that a complex sentence, such as a passive, is stored in memory as a simple, active, declarative sentence, together with a rule which indicates what transformation needs to be applied to the sentence in order to derive the original sentence during recall. While a number of studies initially appeared to support the theory, more recent ones have not, and it cannot be regarded at present as a viable memory model.

Rohrman (1968) has recently proposed another interpretation based on the linguistic model. He suggested that memory for sentences is related directly to the complexity of the deep structure of the sentence. He investigated the problem by comparing memory for English subject nominalizations, such as "growling lions," and object nominalizations, such as "raising flowers," which are identical in surface structure, but differ in their underlying structures. This is illustrated in Fig. 10 in which tree diagrams depict the deep structures of the two nominalizations according to the transformational model. It can be seen that the deep structure of "raising flowers" is the more complex in that it involves an extra node and a missing element (PRO) which is only implicit in the actual surface structure of the nominalization. That is, it is understood that some agent raises flowers, but this is not directly stated. Rohrman presented lists of nominalizations of the two types for immediate free recall and, consistent with his predictions, the subject nominalizations with the simpler deep structures were easier to recall. A later experiment by Rohrman and Polzella (1968) showed that this effect could not be explained in terms of any differences in meaningfulness, and they concluded that sentences are stored in memory in the form of deep structures and that the ease of recalling sentences depends on the complexity of those deep structures. In effect, Rohrman proposed a specific interpretation of semantic effects on memory, semantics or meaning being interpreted in terms of deep structures.

However, Rohrman did not control for the imagery value of the nominalizations. Is it possible that his subject nominalizations exceeded the object nominalizations in imagery, and that this variable was mainly responsible for the observed effect on recall? Rohrman kindly sent me his pool of nominalizations, and I had them rated for their image-arousing value by a group of subjects. It turned out that the subject nominalizations were indeed somewhat higher in imagery on the average than the less easily remembered object nominalizations. To test the possibility that imagery was the effective underlying variable more directly, I repeated the Rohrman recall study with the modification that nominalization type and imagery level were systematically varied in the test lists. That is, the lists

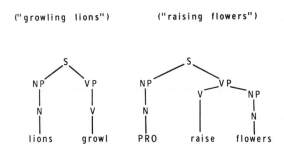

Fig. 10. Tree diagrams showing the deep structures of subject nominalizations ("growling lions") and objects nominalizations ("raising flowers"). Symbols refer to sentence (S), noun phrase (NP), verb phrase (VP), noun (N), and verb (V).

included subject nominalizations that were high imagery as well as ones that were low imagery, and similarly for object nominalizations. The high imagery subject nominalizations were items like *falling stars, dancing girls,* and *reigning kings,* and the low imagery subject nominalizations included *existing situations, clamoring masses,* and *persisting doubts.* High imagery object nominalizations included *mopping floors, ironing clothes,* and *painting pictures.* The low imagery object nominalizations included *hearing rumors, yielding points,* and *keeping secrets.*

The results of a single-trial free recall experiment are shown in Fig. 11. It can be seen that high imagery nominalizations were consistently easier to recall than low imagery nominalizations, but nominalization type had no main effect. Thus Rohrman's deep structure interpretation of his findings was not supported. The

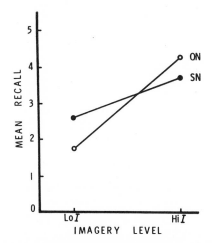

Fig. 11. Mean recall scores for low imagery and high imagery subject (SN) and object (ON) nominalizations.

two variables also interacted in such a manner that recall was better for object nominalizations when the items were high imagery, and for subject nominalizations when they were low imagery. The interaction, however, was relatively small compared to the main effect of imagery. The experiment was repeated twice, using new sets of nominalizations that we had developed ourselves, with essentially the same results: in each case there was a strong positive effect of imagery, but no main effect of nominalization type.

Correlations were also computed between recall scores for the nominalizations and imagery values of the individual words within the nominalizations. The average correlations over 3 experiments are shown in Table 1. Note that nominalization imagery, noun imagery, and participle imagery all correlated significantly with recall, but noun imagery alone was as good, or slightly better, a predictor than nominalization imagery. This suggests that the subject needed only recall the object-image in order to reconstruct the "scene" described by the nominalization as a whole, and from it generate the appropriate verbal output. This is speculative, but presumably testable. In any case, it is clear that the results provide no support for the deep structure interpretation of memory for nominalizations, but they are fully consistent with an interpretation based on the imagery construct, although the precise *modus operandi* of the mechanism remains to be specified.

SUMMARY AND FURTHER EXTENSIONS

I have presented some evidence in support of the theory that imagery can be profitably viewed as an aspect of meaning, or at least as an implicit reaction to verbal stimuli, which mediates such psycholinguistic phenomena as comprehension, retention, and the production of connected discourse. The research obviously needs to be extended in the areas I have touched on here as well as to such important problems as the acquisition of imagery as a response to words, and the possible role of imagery in the early development of language.

TABLE 1

Correlations between Attributes of English Nominalizations
and Free Recall Scores[a]

Attribute	r with recall
Nominalization type	.06
Nominalization imagery	.37
Participle imagery	.23
Noun imagery	.53

[a]Average r over three experiments. Note: $r_{.05} = .20$.

In regard to the first of the above problems, Ronald Philipchalk (1970) has recently demonstrated that nonsense syllable stimuli acquire effective concreteness when pictures or concrete words serve as response items in a paired-associate learning task, effectiveness being defined by the effect of the syllables as stimulus items in a subsequent learning task. Syllables previously paired with pictures were superior to those paired with concrete words which, in turn, surpassed those previously associated with abstract words. However, this occurred only when the subjects were also instructed to use their previous associations in the transfer task, indicating that the mediators needed to be primed. That images indeed served as the mediators was supported by post-learning questionnaire data which indicated that the reported use of images was highest for nonsense syllables paired with pictures, and lowest for those previously paired with abstract words.

The major implication of the imagery approach for language acquisition is that linguistic competence and linguistic performance may be initially dependent upon a substrate of imagery. Through exposure to concrete objects and events, the infant develops a storehouse of images which represent his knowledge of the world. Language builds upon this foundation and remains interlocked with it, although it also develops a partly autonomous structure of its own. Although speculative, these general assumptions would probably arouse little controversy if limited only to discrete objects and their names. An infant indicates by his behavior that he recognizes objects before he responds to the names, thereby showing that he has stored some kind of representation against which the perceptual information is matched. Later he can respond appropriately to the name of an object even in its absence (e.g., he may begin to look for it), indicating the emergence of a word-image relationship. Serious objections might be raised, however, if such an analysis were to be extended to grammatical word sequences, for surely it is too much to suggest that syntax is in any sense built upon a foundation of imagery. Yet this is precisely what I am suggesting.

The argument is as follows.[3] The developing infant is not merely exposed to static objects, but to objects in relation to other objects, and to action sequences involving them. The events and relations are lawful, i.e., they tend to repeat themselves in certain essential respects—people repeatedly enter a room through the same door, in the same way; a bottle is picked up in a predictable way; and so on. In brief, there is a kind of syntax to the observed events, which becomes incorporated into the representational imagery as well. This syntax is elaborated and enriched by the addition of an action component derived from the child's own actions, and these actions have their own patterning or grammar. The child also learns names for the events and relations, as well as the objects involved in them, which we interpret theoretically to mean that associations have developed between

[3] Rather similar views have been presented independently by Osgood in a recent paper entitled "Where do sentences come from?" (1971).

the mental representations of the objects, actions, etc., and their descriptive names. This basic stage becomes greatly elaborated as function words are acquired and as intraverbal associative networks expand through usage. Eventually, abstract verbal skills are attained whereby verbal behavior and verbal understanding are possible at a *relatively* autonomous intraverbal level, i.e., free of dependence not only upon a concrete situational context, but to some extent from imagery as well. Some suggestive evidence for these views has been reviewed elsewhere (Paivio, 1971), but systematic research designed specifically to test their implications remains to be done.

REFERENCES

Atkinson, R. C., & Shiffrin, R. M. Human memory: A proposed system and its control processes. In K. W. Spence and J. T. Spence (Eds.) *The psychology of learning and motivation: Advances in research and theory*. Vol. II. New York: Academic Press, 1968.

Bartlett, F. C. *Remembering*. Cambridge (England): Cambridge University Press, 1932.

Begg, I., & Paivio, A. Concreteness and imagery in sentence meaning. *Journal of Verbal Learning and Verbal Behavior*, 1969, 8, 821-827.

Bousfield, W. A. The problem of meaning in verbal behavior. In C. N. Cofer (Ed.), *Verbal learning and verbal behavior*. New York: McGraw-Hill, 1961.

Bower, G. H. Mental imagery and associative learning. In Lee Gregg (Ed.). *Cognition in learning and memory*. New York: Wiley, 1970.

Bregman, A. S., & Strasberg, R. Memory for the syntactic form of sentences. *Journal of Verbal Learning and Verbal Behavior*, 1968, 7, 396-403.

Brown, R. W. *Words and things*. Glencoe, Ill.: Free Press, 1958.

Bugelski, B. R. Learning theory and the reading process. In *The 23rd annual reading conference*. Pittsburgh: University of Pittsburgh Press, 1969, in press.

Chomsky, N. *Aspects of the theory of syntax*. Cambridge, Mass.: M.I.T. Press, 1965.

Crowder, R. G., & Morton, J. Precategorical acoustic storage (PAS). *Perception and Psychophysics*, 1969, 5, 365-373.

Ernest, C. H., & Paivio, A. Imagery ability in paired-associate and incidental learning. *Psychonomic Science*, 1969, 15, 181-182.

Ernest, C. H., & Paivio, A. Imagery and verbal associative latencies as a function of imagery ability. *Canadian Journal of Psychology*, 1971, 25, 83-90.

Gough, P. B. Grammatical transformations and speed of understanding. *Journal of Verbal Learning and Verbal Behavior*, 1965, 4, 107-111.

Hebb, D. O. *The organization of behavior*. New York: Wiley, 1949.

Huttenlocher, J. Constructing spatial images: A strategy in reasoning. *Psychological Review*, 1968, 75, 550-560.

Miller, G. A. Some psychological studies of grammar. *American Psychologist*, 1962, 17, 748-762.

Moore, T. V. The temporal relations of meaning and imagery. *Psychological Review*, 1915, 22, 177-225.

Neisser, U. *Cognitive psychology*. New York: Appleton, 1967.

Neisser, U. Visual imagery as process and as experience. Paper presented at the Center for Research in Cognition and Affect. New York, June, 1968.

Osgood, C. E. *Method and theory in experimental psychology*. New York: Oxford University Press, 1953.

Osgood, C. E. Where do sentences come from? In D. Steinberg and L. Jakobvits (Eds.), *Semantics: an interdisciplinary reader in philosophy, linguistics, and psychology*. New York: Cambridge University Press, 1971.

Paivio, A. Latency of verbal associations and imagery to noun stimuli as a function of abstractness and generality. *Canadian Journal of Psychology*, 1966, **20**, 378-387.

Paivio, A. A factor-analytic study of word attributes and verbal learning. *Journal of Verbal Learning and Verbal Behavior*, 1968, **7**, 41-49.

Paivio, A. Mental imagery in associative learning and memory. *Psychological Review*, 1969, **76**, 3, 241-263.

Paivio, A. On the functional significance of imagery. In H. W. Reese (Chm.), Imagery in children's learning: A symposium. *Psychological Bulletin*, 1970, **73**, 385-392.

Paivio, A. *Imagery and verbal processes*. New York: Holt, Rinehart & Winston, 1971.

Paivio, A., & Begg, I. Imagery and comprehension latencies as a function of sentence structure and concreteness. Research Bulletin No. 154, Department of Psychology, University of Western Ontario, 1970.

Paivio, A., & O'Neill, B. J. Visual recognition thresholds and dimensions of word meaning. *Perception and Psychophysics*, 1970, **8**, 273-275.

Paivio, A., Yuille, J. C., & Madigan, S. Concreteness, imagery, and meaningfullness values for 925 nouns. *Journal of Experimental Psychology Monograph Supplement*, 1968, **76**, (1, Pt. 2).

Philipchalk, R. The development of imaginal meaning in verbal stimuli. Unpublished doctoral dissertation, University of Western Ontario, 1970.

Philipchalk, R., & Begg, I. Context concreteness and form class in the retention of CVCs. Research Bulletin No. 155, Department of Psychology, University of Western Ontario, 1970.

Pompi, K. F., & Lachman, R. Surrogate processes in the short-term retention of connected discourse. *Journal of Experimental Psychology*, 1967, **75**, 143-150.

Posner, M. I., Boies, S. J., Eichelman, W. H., & Taylor, R. L. Retention of visual and name codes of single letters. *Journal of Experimental Psychology Monograph*, 1969, 79 (1, Pt. 2).

Reese, H. W. Imagery and contextual meaning. In H. W. Reese (Chm.), Imagery in children's learning: A symposium. *Psychological Bulletin*, 1970, **73**, 404-414.

Rohrman, N. L. The role of syntactic structure in the recall of English nominalizations. *Journal of Verbal Learning and Verbal Behavior*, 1968, **7**, 904-912.

Rohrman, N. L., & Polzella, D. J. Recall of subject nominalizations. *Psychonomic Science*, 1968, **12**, 373-374.

Rohwer, W. D., Jr. Images and pictures in children's learning: Research results and instructional implications. In H. W. Reese (Chm.), Imagery in children's learning: A symposium. *Psychological Bulletin*, 1970, **73**, 393-403.

Sachs, J. S. Recognition memory for syntactic and semantic aspects of connected discourse. *Perception and Psychophysics*, 1967, **2**, 437-442. (a)

Sachs, J. S. Recognition of semantic, syntactic and lexical changes in sentences. Paper presented at Psychonomic Society Meetings, October, 1967. Chicago, Ill. (b)

Simpson, H. M. Inferring cognitive processes from pupillary activity and response time. Colloquium presented at the University of Western Ontario, January, 1970.

Sperling, G. The information available in brief visual presentations. *Psychological Monographs*, 1960, 74 (Whole No. 498).

Tversky, B. Pictorial and verbal encoding in a short-term memory task. *Perception and Psychophysics,* 1969, 6, 225-233.

Werner, H., & Kaplan, B. *Symbol formation: an organismic developmental approach to the psychology of language and the expression of thought.* New York: Wiley, 1963.

Wickens, D. D., & Engle, R. W. Imagery and abstractness in short-term memory. *Journal of Experimental Psychology,* 1970, 84, 268-272.

Yuille, J. C., & Paivio, A. Abstractness and the recall of connected discourse. *Journal of Experimental Psychology,* 1969, 82, 3, 467-471.

Yuille, J. C., Paivio, A., & Lambert, W. E. Noun and adjective imagery and order in paired-associate learning by French and English subjects. *Canadian Journal of Psychology,* 1969, 23, 459-466.

CHAPTER 3

WHERE ARE THE VISIONS IN VISUAL PERCEPTION?[1]

Ralph Norman Haber

Nearly all models of visual perception specify in some manner that the patterned optical array reaching the receptor surface is represented by neural elements in the cortex, although the nature of these representations differ from model to model. One point of agreement, however, is that an isomorphism between the receptor and the cortical cells is almost certainly impossible. Granting this, a rather large number of possibilities remain, both at the molecular level and at the level of the conceptual model to be used to explain visual perception.

Since I read George Sperling's dissertation in 1958 (published in 1960), I have been impressed with the possibility that the visual information store he discussed might serve as the first stage of a central representation. This thought has clearly been suggested to others as well, including Sperling (1963, 1967), Neisser (1967), Sternberg (e.g., Sternberg, 1969), and Hochberg (1968, pp. 301-339; 1970), to mention only a few researchers.

I will describe several studies and some speculations of my own about early central representations. These are appropriately included in a book about imagery for several reasons. First, this early central stage has been often referred to as an image, although Neisser (1967) prefers the more neutral term "icon" so as to avoid

[1] The research under my authorship, described in this paper, was supported in part by a research grant from the United States Public Health Service (MH 10753), and three research grants from the National Science Foundation (GB 4547, GB 2909, and GB 5910).

the other or the surplus meanings attached to the concept of an image. Next, as I will try to show later, this early stage does have visual qualities—i.e., perceivers can see their icons.

Sperling's dissertation followed from George Miller's interests on the limits of codable memory (e.g., Miller, 1956). Sperling wanted to know whether this limit was imposed on the reception of stimulation, or whether it occurred at some later stage in memory maintenance or retrieval. The very nature of this limit imposes great difficulty when investigating this question, since one cannot discover how much information the perceiver saw in the stimulus when the latter's report is so restricted. The important contribution that Sperling made was circumventing this limit by using a partial report procedure. In effect, he rediscovered the work of Baxt which had been published in 1871. One display Sperling used was of 12 letters, arranged as 3 rows of 4 letters each. In the base-line condition, the subject is asked to report all that he saw and could remember. In general, the upper limit is between 4 and 6 items correctly reported. In the partial report condition, a tone followed the presentation of the display, its pitch telling the subject whether he was to report the top, middle, or bottom row. Figure 1 briefly illustrates this procedure. Thus, while the subject is presented with 12 items, he is only asked to report 4. Since a total of 4 items is below the memory limit, Sperling assumed that if the subject saw all 4, he should be able to report them without further loss. Consequently, the *percentage* of the 4 that were correctly reported could be used as an estimate of the percentage of the 12 that were perceived by the subject. A typical pattern of results of this procedure (taken from Averbach and Sperling, 1961, pp. 196-211) is illustrated in Fig. 2. Sperling referred to the area under the two curves as the amount of visual information storage. Thus, for a predetermined brief period of time after the display ended the tone permitted the subject to report much more visual information than he could have if he had attempted to report everything he had seen.

Sperling referred to this as a *visual* information storage for several reasons. He assumed that it was a visual representation because his subjects said that they felt as if, for a fraction of second, they could *see* the entire display before it faded, even though they could *report* only a small part of it when asked to report all of it. In

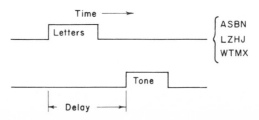

Fig. 1. Sequence of stimuli in partial report procedure. *S* reports only the row indicated by pitch of tone.

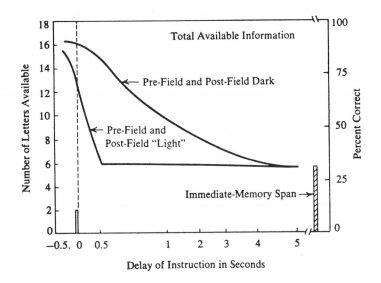

Fig. 2. Results of a partial report procedure. The abscissa is the delay between the onset of the array of letters and the onset of the indicator. [From Averbach and Sperling (1961).]

addition, in the dark adaptation condition, visual storage was much longer. These findings led Sperling to speculate that the visual information storage might be similar to a visual afterimage.

In the 12 years since Sperling's thesis was completed, there have been a large number of replications of a visual storage effect using the partial report procedure. A substantial review of these replications was carried out by Neisser in 1967, although his review badly needs updating. To mention only one of these earlier studies, the most extensive was made by Averbach and Coriell (1961). Their displays were 2 rows of 8 letters, each with a visual post-stimulus indicator (rather than a tone) to cue the subject. A bar marker appeared above a letter in the top row, or below a letter in the bottom row, and the subject was to report only that particular 1 of the 16 letters. They made the same assumption that Sperling did—that the probability of correctly reporting the indicated letter would be an estimate of the percentage of letters available in visual storage at the time the indicator arrived. They found that for a light-adapted testing situation visual storage ended by about 250 milliseconds. This time span was arrived at through several variations of the experiment and is acknowledged to be a fairly reliable estimate.

In the subsequent work by Sperling and in the very fine discussion in Neisser's book (1967), the notion of a visual information storage has played a growing role in the attempts to understand visual perception of codable stimuli. However, there have been two questions substantially overlooked in all of these experiments and discussions, and it is to these problems that I wish to devote most of this chapter. First, the researcher asks whether this visual storage is in fact *visual*. Is it an image? Can the perceiver see it? Does it contain information that is visual in nature?

The second question is at a very different level, but critical to the role such visual storage might play in the processing of visually presented information. Since the natural world is devoid of tachistoscopes and tachistoscopic displays of stimuli (the only reasonable exception occurs when one attempts to read during a lightning storm—behavior I do not consider very natural), what practical use can there be in having a brief image or icon, when the stimulus that created it remains continuously on view? An unsatisfactory answer to this question implies that we may have discovered a phenomenon in the laboratory which has no parallel in real life. I feel that there are very satisfactory answers to the second question; in fact, these answers are directly connected with the assumptions made during the study of visual perception.

Before turning to the first of these two questions, I would like to summarize what I believe the properties of an iconic storage are, though I will not cite all of the supporting evidence for each statement.

PROPERTIES OF ICONIC STORAGE

An iconic representation is the first central stage in information extraction or the processing of visual stimulation. The icon develops shortly after stimulus onset and continues while the stimulus pattern remains on each of the retinae. After the stimulus ends or changes, its icon persists briefly, although it finally fades away. Thus, while the initial evidence demonstrating the existence of an icon used very brief stimuli, so that the persistence of the icon could be ascertained, I assume that the icon is also present during the stimulus exposure regardless of whether the stimulus is brief or long.

After the stimulus terminated the duration of the persistence of the icon was estimated by Averbach and Coriell to be about ¼ second, a time span that recurred in several other studies. This estimate is, however, open to several qualifications.

Eriksen (1970) has suggested that the estimate of persistence is too low when obtained from a partial-report experiment. He argues that it takes a certain amount of time for the perceiver to locate and process the indicator. This time should be added to the estimate of the duration of the icon. His experiments suggest that a minimum of another 100 milliseconds is involved in such processing. Further, an unpublished work at Rochester by Dick and Lefton (1970) has shown that the decay function is shallower and starts from a higher point with an auditory (as compared to a visual) indicator, suggesting that the auditory indicator is processed more rapidly. While Sperling felt that the persistence of the icon is relatively independent of stimulus duration, I will present some data later which suggests that the persistence is negatively correlated with stimulus duration—only brief flashes have persisting icons. It appears that the luminance of the flash does not appreciably affect the icon's duration. However, the adaptation state of the eye has an enormous effect. Sperling in his dissertation showed a fivefold to tenfold increase in the duration of visual storage when the eye is dark adapted. It was this effect which suggested to him that the visual information storage might be like an afterimage. Many other experiments have verified the substantial increase under dark-adaptation conditions. It should be noted that just as reading in a lightning storm is unusual, to say the least, the normal environment rarely presents information to the dark-adapted eye. Thus, the more typical circumstance found in information processing situations of all kinds involves a light-adapted eye. Here the evidence suggests that the amount of ambient illumination does not have an appreciable effect.

The content of the icon has been thought by some to be photographic in the sense that all the information contained in the stimulus was contained in the icon. Given the possibility that the icon was due simply to an afterimage, this assumption had a certain plausibility. Sperling did not necessarily accept all of the meanings of the photographic metaphor, however, and Neisser preferred the term iconic to avoid words such as "image" or "photographic representation." My feeling is that the analogy to an afterimage is a poor one. Rather, I think that the icon contains those features that have been extracted from the stimulus by feature-detector processes that occur between the retina and the cortex. The most likely detector processes are those arising from the various types of receptive field organizations. Thus, the features available to man would be only lines, angles, orientations, velocities, color, and retinal disparity. Certainly the long series of experiments on many different kinds of animals by Hubel, Wiesel, and others have not uncovered any other features besides these. The detail and resolution of these features would depend upon the retinal distribution of receptive fields. Stimuli that fall near the fovea probably will have more precise features extracted than those formed in the periphery of the retina. Perhaps as we know the distribution of receptive fields across the human retina better, we will have a clearer idea of the kind of information available to peripheral vision, and how it is initially represented.

The rate of establishment of the icon is not known. I assume that it is quite rapid, probably similar to the length of time it takes information to travel from the eye to the brain. Further, I assume that these features are all extracted in parallel, that is, the information comes from each receptive field at the same time.

No influence of memory, prior learning, expectation, set, or the like should occur in the extraction of visual features. Thus, the content of iconic storage would appear to be an unorganized collection of primitive features of the visual field.

Sperling assumed that the visual information storage is visual, implying that the perceiver could see the features in his icon. It is important to note that while the icon may be visible to the perceiver (I will discuss evidence on this below) he should not know what it contains until be processes its content further. The features represented are primitive and are not classified under meanings, or organizations. In fact, if the current theorizing of Neisser (1967) and Hochberg (1968, 1970) is correct, even basic figure-ground segregation and the Gestalt laws of organization are not features of the icon but are the result of subsequent processing of those features.

Information extraction from the icon is assumed to be an active process, heavily under control of schemas and programs derived from prior experience, expectancies, and familiarity with the stimuli. Sperling (1963) argued that linguistic information is extracted serially and the features composing each letter in the stimulus are combined into labels one by one. He further assumed that for most alphabetic material the items are encoded in a left-to-right fashion, so that the features that make up the leftmost letter of a string of letters would be processed first. Then that leftmost letter would be named, and so forth.

There is a substantial amount of evidence now which shows that Sperling is basically correct in his suppositions, though much of the detail of this information extraction process is yet to be explained. Before reviewing this evidence, let me mention that the naming of items is not the only processing that would normally occur, even for linguistic stimuli. For example, a classification test (e.g., Posner and Mitchell, 1967) may ask the perceiver to decide only whether two visual forms are identical or not. In this case he does not have to name them and, in fact, probably does not know their names at the time he is able to decide whether they are the same or not—the visual match presumably being made among the as yet unnamed features. To do this might still require additional steps beyond the mere presence of the features themselves, but it would not require processing as extensive as that needed to attach names to these features. Posner's multiple classification system clearly makes this distinction. In addition to comparing visual forms, the perceiver's task might be to look for the presence (or absence) of a feature, to match a set of features against features in memory, to extract and then match the name of the features against names stored in memory, or to search through a group of features looking for a particular pattern of features. All of these are information extraction processes that operate after the icon has been created.

As an example of one experimental design used to study processing rates, Sperling (1963) presented the subject with a linear array of letters for a varying duration, immediately following their termination with visual noise, designed to erase or to so interfere with the icon that the information extraction from it had to cease. Figure 3 shows the results of that experiment. In it he finds that for each 10 milliseconds during which the stimulus is available before it is masked, the subject is capable of processing (i.e., correctly reporting) 1 additional letter. If the subject is dark adapted prior to the flash, then apparently the icon is formed quickly and processing can begin immediately. If the prior adaptation state contains a noise field in it, then it takes the subject 20 or 30 milliseconds before he can begin processing. The rate of 10 milliseconds per item in this type of task has been found by Scharf and Lefton (1970), and has been found in several studies in my own laboratory (e.g., Haber, Standing and Boss, 1972) as well as in several others in the literature.

This brief survey on the nature of iconic storage is far from complete and very poorly documented. I hope it does highlight some of its characteristics and provide a background for consideration of the two questions about iconic storage that I raised earlier.

IS THE ICON VISIBLE?

Most of the evidence suggesting that there is an iconic storage has been indirect, based on the amount of information the perceiver has available after the

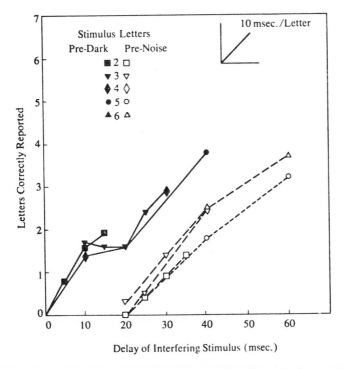

Fig. 3. Number of letters reported as a function of time from stimulus onset to onset of visual noise. The curves to the left are for a dark-adapted subject while those to the right adapted the subject to a visual noise field. [From Sperling (1963).]

supposed icon has faded. I wanted to develop tests that were more direct—tests that ask the perceiver to describe some properties of his icon while it is still present.

Lionel Standing, as a Research Associate at Rochester for 2 years, conducted several experiments on this with me. The problem we faced was that the icon is too brief for us to directly ask the subject how long it persisted. With suitable adjustment in intensity, for example, flashes of 10^{-9} seconds can appear to be as long as flashes of 10^{-2} seconds, a difference of 7 log units, suggesting that we could not rely on judgments of absolute duration. We explored 3 alternative procedures which avoided partial reports.

One procedure (Haber and Standing, 1969) involved recycling the light flash. As an analogy, imagine that you are to operate an incandescent light bulb with the instruction to turn it on momentarily, and then on again as soon as the filament appears to have faded completely—several seconds for most incandescent lights. If a timer is attached to the light switch, the resultant pattern of on—off intervals will show that you turned the switch on briefly every several seconds. The interval between the "on" switches would be a measure of the visual persistence of the filament in the light bulb, plus whatever persistence there might be in the measuring instrument—your eye. We ran this same experiment, except that we used a light which had a negligible persistence (only a few microseconds). Consequently, if there was any apparent persistence, it would be in the eye and not in the light. Figure 4 illustrates the procedure. A black outline figure on a white background was briefly presented in 1 channel of a tachistoscope (12½ milliseconds was our standard condition), followed by a variable "off" time in which a blank, white adaptation field replaced the stimulus field. These 2 channels continued to alternate for a number of cycles. The subject's task was to watch the 2 fields and decide whether the black outline form completely faded (or disappeared) between each of its flashes or whether it appeared to persist such that when it came on again

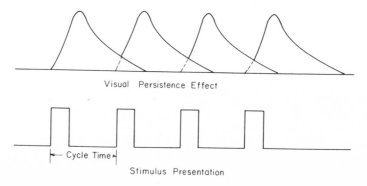

Visual Persistence Effect

|← Cycle Time →|

Stimulus Presentation

Fig. 4. Recycling procedure. The lower trace represents the changes in the stimulus. The upper one represents a hypothetical pattern of persistence. [From Haber and Standing (1969).]

it had not completely disappeared from the previous flash. If he said it had disappeared, then the experimenter shortened the interflash period until a point was located for which it had just disappeared. Following appropriate psychophysical procedures, we then could locate the persistence of the visual form. Figure 5 shows the results over several conditions based on 10 subjects. When the subject is light adapted to a fairly high level of illumination (as when reading) ¼ second must be interposed between flashes for the subject to say that the flash had just faded. Decreasing the amount of light by 2 log units only slightly increases the persistence. Dark adapting the subject, on the other hand, so that the adaptation field is turned off, nearly doubles the persistence, an effect reminiscent of those from the partial report measures of iconic storage. Hence, it seems that persistence is not very dependent upon the level of illumination, but that it is highly dependent upon the adaptation level. In another condition, we presented alternate flashes dichoptically to each eye. If the persistence is entirely retinal, that is, not only is it generated retinally, but it is being monitored by the subject retinally, then the flashes to each eye would have to come 250 milliseconds apart for the subject to say that the figure had just faded. Since only every other flash comes to the same eye, the rate of flashing would have to be doubled. On the other hand, if the persistence is measured centrally, then no change in the rate of flashing would be needed even with dichoptic presentations. The latter effect was found because the dichoptic presentations required the same rate. Thus, while the persistence may be generated retinally, though there is no reason to assume that it is, the perceiver's judgment of

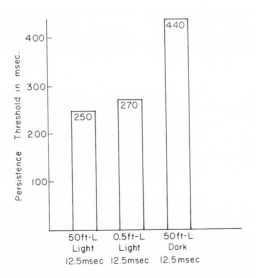

Fig. 5. Stimulus presentation of a black circle. Bar graphs showing the persistence of an outline figure under various recycling conditions. [From Haber and Standing (1969).]

the persistence must be occurring at some point after the information from both eyes has been combined.

We have used this experimental design with a number of other stimuli, including rare words and familiar words. The effects have been virtually identical, suggesting that the content of the stimulus or its meaningfulness is not a relevant variable to its persistence.

A second procedure used to observe visual storage was initially worked out by Haber and Nathanson (1968) and extended by Haber and Standing (1969). The subject was instructed to look at an outline figure that he had to view through a vertical slit $1/8$ inch wide, which oscillated back and forth in front of the figure. Thus, at any instant in time only a small fraction of the figure was on view—that which could be seen through the slit. Since, in this procedure, the subject tended to fixate some particular part of the figure, when the slit was set in very high oscillatory motion, such that, for example, only 50 milliseconds elapsed from the time the left part of the figure was viewed until the right part of the figure was exposed, then the figure was painted across the retina in only 50 milliseconds. Subjects universally report that in this condition they can see the entire figure and that its contours are fairly sharp. The faster the slit is set in motion, the darker the contours, approaching the sharpness of the perceived contours when the figure is seen in its entirety.

The experimental procedure was to vary the speed of oscillation and ask the subject at each speed whether the entire figure could be seen, or whether while one end was sharply in view (because the slit had just swept over it), the other end of the figure had faded from view. Following a psychophysical procedure similar to that in the previous experiment, we determined the speed of oscillation necessary for the subject to view the entire figure without part of it fading while another part remained sharp. This duration for 10 subjects was about 280 milliseconds under normal room illumination, and it increased to 300 milliseconds in very dim illumination, estimates of iconic persistence no more than 10% greater than that found for the recycling procedure.

A third experimental procedure that we have used (Haber and Standing, 1970) follows a design initially suggested by Sperling (1967). The subject observes a flash of light. Coincident with its onset, he hears a very brief click. The subject is told that every few seconds he will again see and hear the paired flash-click. Between the presentations of each pair the subject is free to adjust a timer which will change the relative asynchrony of the flash and the click, such that if the subject judges that the click came before the flash, he can adjust their asynchrony so that on the next flash the click is delayed relative to the flash. The subject views the pairs often enough to make a satisfactory onset simultaneity match. Then the click is set to occur near the offset of the flash and the subject is again asked to make a series of judgments until he has set the click to be simultaneous with the offset of the flash. Figure 6 illustrates the experimental design. Our assumption is

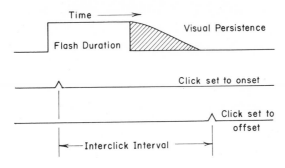

Persistence = Interclick Interval - Flash Duration

Fig. 6.   Sequence of stimuli in a flash-click study. [From Haber and Standing (1970).]

that the interclick interval calculated from these two sets of judgments would be an index of the apparent duration of the stimulus, plus any persistence. If there is no persistence at all, that is, if the subject thinks the stimulus terminates simultaneously with its physical termination, then the interclick interval should equal the physical duration of the stimulus. On the other hand, if the subject feels that a 50 millisecond stimulus persisted for 200 milliseconds after it was physically turned off, he should set the interclick interval at 250 milliseconds. Our subjects, after some practice, found this a relatively easy task, because they noted that when they felt the click and the flash coincided just right, they also had a feeling of apparent causality between the two. Once this perception occurred, the standard deviation of their judgments was very small.

Figure 7 reports the results for the condition in which the subject is light adapted before and after the flash and when he is dark adapted. Here the picture is slightly different from the previous studies. If the flash is very brief, under 30 or 40 milliseconds, the light adapted subject adds a persistence of nearly 200 milliseconds and the dark adapted subject nearly 400 milliseconds. However, if the flash is longer, the amount of persistence is much less, until, by the time the flash is itself ¼ or ½ second the amount of persistence becomes negligible. Hence, only brief flashes appear to have any persistence. This finding becomes important in my discussion later.

One further question was investigated in this study. Sperling (1963) and Averbach and Coriell (1961) argued that iconic storage should be erasable. A number of mechanisms have been proposed for this type of process, but the simplest explanation is that a subsequent stimulus creates its own icon which replaces the icon of the previous stimulation. This is discussed in some detail by Neisser (1967). Since we were concerned with the visual characteristics of iconic storage, we ran an additional condition in which a mask followed the display after a delay. Figure 8 shows the results. Since the parameter in the figure is the delay from

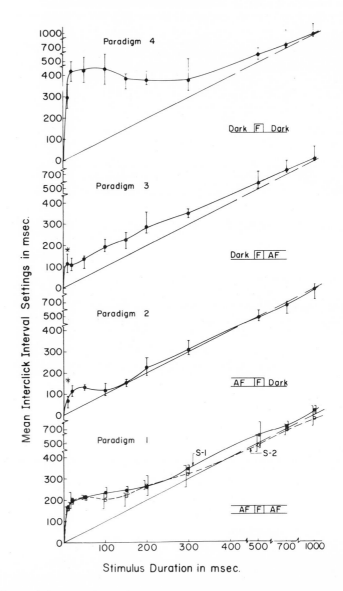

Fig. 7. Some of the results from a flash-click study showing the change in the apparent duration of the flash (interclick interval) as a function of flash duration for several conditions. [From Haber and Standing (1970).]

the onset of the stimulus until the onset of the mask, it is clear that the onset of the mask terminates the persistence rather precisely, since all of the points tend to fall along straight lines of zero slope. The only deviation is for those values correspond-

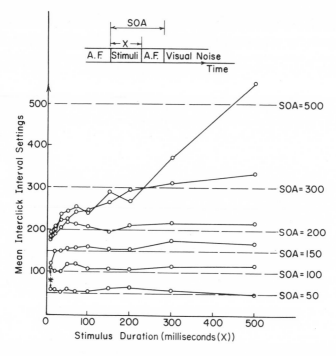

Fig. 8. The effect of following the stimulus with visual noise on the interclick interval. [From Haber and Standing (1970).]

ing to persistences that have already faded. Thus, brief flashes have a persistence of just less than 200 milliseconds. If the mask arrives after 200 milliseconds the persistence has ended by itself and the subject will set the interclick interval at less than the interval between the stimulus onset and the mask onset. What is most noteworthy is that there are no exceptions to the general principle that the mask will terminate the persistence of a target if the mask arrives before the normal persistence ends of its own accord. The mask has no impact at all on the persistence if the persistence has ended.

Therefore, the answer to the first question appears to be clear. Yes—visual information storage, or iconic storage, is visual, even though it is brief. Since all the experiments reviewed above require the subject to report some visual characteristic of iconic storage, it follows that he can see something in his icon.

Before turning to the second question, it might be interesting to speculate as to what it is that the subject sees; the experiments just reviewed do not tell us this. In terms of the general model being presented here, however, I suggest that he does not know what he sees; meaning that he can tell that there is something out there, but at that point in time he has not performed any analysis, integration, or labeling, so that the material is uncoded, unidentified, unrecognized, and unfamiliar. A frequent comment made by subjects in all of the experiments we have run is about the unknowability of brief inputs. If the stimulus is terminated abruptly by visual noise, but had been bright and with good contrast, subjects will say that they saw the stimulus clearly, but they did not have enough time to recognize it.

We ran an experiment (Haber and Standing, 1968) in which on some trials the subject was asked to rate the clarity (that is, the sharpness of the contrast) of some letters that were briefly presented. On other trials he was asked to recognize the letters. The letters were presented for a fixed duration which, if they had not been followed by visual noise, would have been adequate for a high clarity rating and for perfect recognition. However, visual noise followed the items after variable delays. What we found was that for very brief delay intervals the subjects would report that the clarity had already achieved a high level, even though in the other condition at the same interval they were unable to perform much above chance on recognition. Hence, experimentally we have demonstrated that they could see the letters clearly but were unable to recognize them.

WHAT FUNCTION DOES ICONIC STORAGE SERVE?

Let me then turn to the second question: How can a briefly persisting icon be of any use when there are no tachistoscopically presented stimuli in the normal environment? The question is quite reasonable, and it has been asked by many persons. However, posing it in this way suggests some critical misunderstanding that Hochberg (e.g., Hochberg, 1970), Neisser (e.g., Neisser, 1967), and Kolers (e.g., Kolers, 1969) have worked hardest to dispel. I hope I can join them in clarifying the problem.

I have assumed that extracted features are the initial representations for all stimuli and that this processing begins and continues while the stimulus is on view. There is no reason to believe that we see photographically for long stimuli and iconically for brief ones. Thus, we always have icons. It is the first central stage. The persistence of iconic representation after the termination of stimulation *is* a function of duration of exposure. Thus, Sperling was wrong, but in a surprising direction—short stimuli have long persistences and long stimuli have short ones. What this does is to permit the stimulus representations to persist long enough to have an effective duration of ¼ second. If the stimulus exposure is longer than that, then the persistence is not relevant. If the subject is dark-adapted prior to exposure, persistence is much longer, but its relation to stimulus exposure is the same. These results seem patently obvious now, after the fact. There is no need for any post-exposure persistence unless the stimulus exposure itself is brief.

These implications become relevant when one recognizes another obvious factor. While the world around us has few tachistoscopically presented stimuli, we do not look at stimuli in the visual world for long periods of time, nor continuously, nor in the entirety. The average duration of fixation in reading is about 250 milliseconds. The average duration of fixation in a visual exploration of the environment is not much longer than that. Hence, we are always extracting information from briefly viewed stimuli. The similarity of these viewing times to the duration of persistence of features measured in the laboratory cannot be a coincidence.

Hochberg has recognized another critical implication of the way we extract information. Perceivers do not, and cannot, see an entire visual field in a single glance. It takes many glances and we never make enough of them. Much of the visual field is never looked at directly and is never seen in clear vision. Hence, an integrated view of a continuous world that we perceive must be *constructed* out of many glances, and all that we know about the visual world around us is constructed out of the information contained in icons. Hochberg even argues that a figure-ground segregation, something that has usually been thought of as the most primitive visual organization, is constructed. It must be constructed, he says, because we usually cannot see an entire figure on a ground in a single glance; rather, it takes several glances. Therefore, it cannot be a primitive feature, but one that is constructed or derived—a result of the integration of several glances.

The icon plays a leading role in this construction, because it is the initial representation of the information in the stimulus. From it we label the information, construct more central representations in other forms, and then go on to the next glance, building up a constructed picture of the world. Adult perceivers apparently need about ¼ second to do all of the processing from the icon before they go on to the next stimulus. What accounts for this invariance is not yet known (at least in detail). I am sure, however, that as we examine visual information tasks such as reading, scanning, or recognition, this time factor will be found in each. It may be the result of how long it takes to process up to some limit, or it may be due to some sensory variables. We need to know this.

Even now, however, it seems clear to me that icons persist beyond stimulus termination, only to guarantee to the perceiver this ¼ second processing time. If he has that time already, no further persistence is needed.

I apologize for so briefly discussing this examination of visual perception and the related model of information processing. Primarily, this chapter is concerned with the end of a sensory peripheral encoding, through the first central stage. The important point to me is that we have a *visual* representation of the features (probably geometric) contained in stimuli. This visual (or iconic) representation is all that is available for further processing.

I have always been interested in possible distinctions between what a perceiver sees and what he constructs. If I am correct in my analysis, this distinction is still critical, but it would be a mistake to suggest that the perceiver knows what he sees, as something beyond what he constructs. While a perceiver may see the world before he knows it, at that early stage of processing he does not know what he sees. Thus, in the beginning there is the image even before the word.

REFERENCES

Averbach, E., & Coriell, A. S. Short-term memory in vision. *Bell System Technical Journal,* 1961, **40**, 309-328.
Averbach, E., & Sperling, G. Short-term storage of information in vision. In C. Cherry (Ed.), *Information theory.* London: Butterworths, 1961.
Baxt, N. Neber die Zeit welche nötig ist, damit ein Gesichtseindruck zum Bewusstein Rommt und über die Grosse (Extension) der bewussten Wahrnehmung bei einem Gesichtseindrucke von gegenebener Dauer. *Pflungers Archives Gesamte Psychologie,* 1871, **4**, 325-336.
Dick, A. O., & Lefton, L. A. Unpublished work, 1970.
Eriksen, C. W. Colloquium presentation, Center for Visual Science, University of Rochester, February, 1970.
Haber, R. N., & Nathanson, L. S. Post-retinal storage? —Parks' camel as seen through the eye of a needle. *Perception and Psychophysics,* 1968, **3**, 349-355.
Haber, R. N., & Standing, L. Clarity and recognition of masked and degraded stimuli. *Psychonomic Science,* 1968, **13**, 83-84.
Haber, R. N., & Standing, L. Direct measures of short-term visual storage. *Quarterly Journal of Experimental Psychology,* 1969, **21**, 43-54.
Haber, R. N., & Standing, L. Direct estimates of apparent duration of a flash followed by visual noise. *Canadian Journal of Psychology,* 1970, **24**, 216-229.
Haber, R. N., Standing, L., & Boss, J. Extraction of letter information from brief visual displays. To be submitted for publication, 1972.
Hochberg, J. In the mind's eye. In R. N. Haber (Ed.), *Contemporary theory and research in visual perception.* New York: Holt, 1968.
Hochberg, J. Attention, organization and consciousness. In D. Mostofsky (Ed.) *Attention: Contemporary theory and analysis,* 1970.
Kolers, P. A. Three stages of reading. In H. Levin and J. Williams (Eds.), *Basic studies in reading.* New York: Harper, 1969.
Miller, G. A. The magical number seven, plus or minus two. *Psychological Review,* 1956, **63**, 81-97.
Neisser, U. *Cognitive psychology.* New York: Appleton, 1967.
Posner, M. I., & Mitchell, R. F. Chronometric analysis of classification. *Psychological Review,* 1967, **74**, 392-409.
Scharf, B., & Lefton, L. A. Backward and forward masking as a function of stimulus and task parameters. *Journal of Experimental Psychology,* 1970, **84**, 331-338.
Sperling, G. The information available in brief visual presentations. *Psychological Monographs,* 1960, **74**, No. 11.
Sperling, G. A model for visual memory tasks. *Human Factors,* 1963, **5**, 19-31.
Sperling, G. Successive approximations to a model for short-term memory. *Acta Psychologica,* 1967, **27**, 285-292.
Sternberg, S. Memory scanning: Mental processes revealed by reaction time experiments. *American Scientist,* 1969, **57**, 421-457.

CHAPTER 4

THE DEFINITION OF THE IMAGE

B. R. Bugelski

The title of this chapter shows how confusing our language is, a point to which I will return later. The title is indeed correct, but the reader's interpretation of it is probably not the intended one. I do not propose to define the image, though the topic "defining an image" will be discussed. I will consider different theoretical views on the definition of an image in the first half and subsequently some empirical approaches.

In recent years we have been exposed to a variety of subjective excursions into what are coming to be acceptably regarded as "cognitive processes." I am not sure that I know what such processes are, and I think that we had best be on our guard against lowering the bars to the entry of unfounded or ill-founded hypothetical constructs into our psychological vocabulary without a careful examination.

Fifty years ago Watson (1913) warned us about subjective approaches to a science. Today, psychologists are again beginning to show no concern about using such terms as "subjective organization (Tulving, 1962)," "plans," and "strategies (Miller, Galanter, and Pribram, 1960)." "Mental processes" and "minds" are referred to by so many as hardly to require citation. The title of a recent work is *Mental Imagery* (Richardson, 1969), and I. E. Farber (1968, p. 149) has stated that "no one these days denies the existence of mental events."[1] Psychoanalysts, starting with Freud, have always been interested in imagery. Modern analysts are making considerable use of imagery reports as compared to simple free verbal associations (see Horowitz, 1969).

Every 50 years or so it might be worthwhile to stop and examine our thinking about the nature of science. The current popularity of work with imagery prompts me to this review of what Watson once referred to as the "ghosts of sensation (1924)." In the light of the great and growing interest in working with imagery, we must be sure that we do not violate generally accepted canons of science. Scientists do not study "ghosts" of any kind. Are we secure in our views that we are not working with figments of imagination or with what Skinner has called "linguistic fictions?" The Polish logician, Kotarbinski, calls these "Onamatoids," and suggests dispensing with mental processes and limiting our attention to things which can be observed by the senses. If images do not exist as *things,* can they exist at all?

Something may exist to which the term "image" has been applied, but a process of translation, sometimes a long one, must be applied before we can come to scientific grips with what we can observe and what we postulate. Before we begin to translate the meaning of imagery, however, there are some questions that must be answered.

Why did Watson discard imagery and why were psychologists so reluctant to study images for so many years; And, again, why has the image recaptured the interest of so many investigators today?

In 1949 Hebb offered an explanation of why the S–R psychologists of the 1930's and 1940's had been so preoccupied with rat research. He pointed out that their basic assumption about the activity of the central nervous system, namely, that it functioned as a connective device in the manner of a telephone switchboard, was perfectly suited to the view that stimuli evoked responses via central connections. The central mechanisms had no other role to play. Such a static description of neural function was almost true of the rat. The rat, according to Hebb, is a stimulus–response animal.

Watson's knowledge of neural activity was rather meager. In his day one had not yet heard of brain waves, of spontaneous neural discharges, and of the reticular activating system. In 1928, 1 year before Berger published his first paper on brain waves, Watson stated (p. 75): "The behaviorist . . . founds his systems upon the belief supported at every point by known facts of physiology that *the brain is stimulated*[2] *always and only from the outside by a sense organ process.*" Such a view, quite literally, did not allow for any independent internal neural reaction or

---

[1] Karel Lambert at a recent symposium at the University of West Virginia commented on this statement to the effect that believing something is hardly the same as having it so. (West Virginia Symposium on Cognitive Processes, 1970.)

[2] Italics are Watson's. *The ways of behaviorism,* New York: Harper, 1928.

internally aroused process (except for kinesthetic stimulation). Watson asserted exactly what Hebb accused the rat psychologists of assuming; Watson rejected the concept that the nervous system had at least limited independence. Having asserted such a view, Watson could hardly countenance anything like an image. Presumably, we now know better. We need no longer be bound by a static nervous system. This freedom, however, does not extend to laying claims to mentalistic phenomena; and, as will be shown, our knowledge of neurophysiology is not yet adequate to permit the translation of imagery into neural terms. I think we know now why Watson was unable to include imagery in his psychology. The next question, about the hiatus in imagery research from the 1920's through the 1950's, is more easily answered—the objective post-Watson psychologists were sweeping the field with great promises of some kind of new order. The promises of the behaviorists remained, alas, unfulfilled; and the post-World War II disillusionment with the lack of success of learning theorists in developing a viable and educationally useful learning theory led to a new preoccupation with formerly shunned cognitive aspects of behavior. Psychologists, at long last, came to study more distinctly human operations like verbal behavior. What is more, the verbal behavior involved real words. The nonsense syllable had had its day. The recognition that paired-associates were being learned by some kinds of mediational processes rather than as simple S–R connections initiated the new wave of research into internal processes. It was not long before psychologists began, tentatively, to talk about images. Today we are taking images very seriously indeed. Thus, our third question is answered.

But we still do not know what we are talking about. We tell people to image something and they tell us they have done so. We use such instructions as operational definitions of imagery when we only describe what *we* are doing. The question of what goes on within the subjects remains unanswered. The problem of definition must now be faced.

At the very outset we find ourselves in a dilemma. It may be that to define something calls for the arousal of images! Consider the case where someone reads the word "panache" and says he does not understand it. He consults the dictionary and reads: "a feather, a bunch of feathers attached to a knight's helmet." He can now resume his reading with some degree of adjustment. We can argue that he has had an image of feathers, helmets, knights, jousts, ladies fair, etc. The meaning of panache resides, we say, in the imagery and attendant emotional reactions.

But, how do you define an image? Does an image engender imagery and attendant emotional reactions? Can you have an image of an image? The word image does not refer to a concrete object; in fact, it does not refer to any object at all, and if we believe that for anything at all to be, it must be in some form or structure, we have to admit that we know nothing about any form or structure that an image might possess or reside in. The need for an object or concrete form has led to the widespread usage of expressions such as pictures in the mind, seeing something with the mind's eye, "impressions made upon a plastic substance (Titchener, 1921)," or in Kluver's more colorful language: "the petrified product of (perceptual) functions (1932)." Because we know nothing about minds or mind's eyes, or "impressions," plastic or petrified in our heads, we recognize these suggestions to be of no scientific value.

The almost universal willingness of people to report that they do have and enjoy (or fear) their images, however, argues for the occurrence of something inside people's heads that generates such reports. Either they have images or they are, as Watson put it, quite deluded. If a vast majority of mankind is, in fact, deluded, then as Margaret Washburn (1916) said, ". . . one might think, a scientific investigator would feel some curiosity regarding the cause of so wide-spread a delusion."

The problem of defining images is not essentially different from the problems commonly faced by psychologists in defining many of their working concepts like *intelligence, habit, drive, personality,* or *cognitive dissonance.* The general approach to definition of such hypothetical constructs or concepts is that of operationism which, in the words of Hull, tries to "anchor" such assumed mechanisms, devices, states, or processes at both ends of an S–R sequence—by spelling out the procedures and measurements applied to the independent and dependent variables under study. In practise, the operational procedure specifies certain conditions under which some alleged phenomenon, process, or state can be postulated to exist. We can examine some of the attempts offered in this context and determine our own degree of satisfaction with the results (Koch, 1954).

In *Mental Imagery,* Richardson (1969) reviews some classical definitions and offers his own, a four-part statement, the first two labeled subjective, the latter two objective. He says:

> Mental imagery refers to (1) all those quasi-sensory or quasi-perceptual experiences of which (2) we are self-consciously aware, and which (3) exist for us in the absence of those stimulus conditions that are known to produce their genuine sensory or perceptual counterparts, and which (4) may be expected to have different consequences from their sensory or perceptual counterparts.

Having read this definition we are no closer to understanding the concept because Richardson asks us to accept some kind of conscious experience as the criterion for imagery without having the latter clarified for us. This definition specifies that external stimuli are not present during the conscious experience, but the reaction is in some way similar to what it would have been if the external stimuli were present. Richardson does go on to consider each point of his definition, but we do not get much beyond the concept of a mental experience from his effort, although his fourth point seems to suggest the use of behavioral consequences as objective criteria.

The attempt by Leuba (1940), endorsed by Mowrer (1960) and partially by Paivio (1969), to define images as conditioned sensations is not much more helpful without a definition of sensations. Conditioning, itself, is definable as a procedure.

However, the sensation, unless we accept Woodworth's old definition as "the first response of the brain to a stimulus" is not definable in objective terminology. But Leuba does make room for the role of external stimuli in generating imagery, something Richardson did not consider. What he does is to allow for new stimuli to generate old sensations or we might put it thus: A stimulus *(A)* not originally effective in generating some response normally elicitable by another stimulus *(B)* can come, through conditioning, to elicit the response evoked by *(B)* or at least, something like it. After a light *(A)* has been paired with a tone *(B)* many times, the light alone comes to elicit a report that the subject "hears" the tone. This imaged or hallucinated tone in response to the light is, for Leuba, a conditioned sensation and the prototype of imagery. But to define the image, it is still necessary to define the conditioned response to the light *(A)*. We know only that the subject reports hearing the tone. We cannot be sure that his experience resembles the unconditioned response to the tone. It does not seem that the conditioned response, as defined in Leuba's experiment with hypnotized subjects, is clear enough to provide a satisfactory definition of imagery.

The notion of conditioning as advanced by Leuba was inherent in Margaret Washburn's (1916) account of imagery which was based on the proposition that imagery, like sensation, occurs when a motor response to some external stimulus is inhibited or blocked. In the case of imagery, a given motor center must have a history of excitation by other sensory centers. When a motor response is blocked, impulses diverted from the motor center can spread out to these other sensory centers and initiate activity therein from what amounts to a central source. Because the motor blockage may not be complete, there may be some incipient movement and kinesthetic stimulation. This may be fed back into the nervous system, and can also initiate imagery by exciting related sensory centers.

Washburn's neurophysiology was somewhat less than sophisticated but her theory called attention to the possible role of conditioning, to inhibited movement, and to kinesthetic feedback from partial motor activity, all of which we will have occasion to consider.

What other characteristics can we attribute to imagery? The responses involved in imagery are inferred, hypothetical, implicit, and internal, not observable by normal visual inspection of the responder. They are reported by the responder as localized in the head; they are not projected into the external world and are not identified as existing externally, as are hallucinations. Perky's classic study (1910) was really a study of hallucination and not of imagery. Her subjects failed to discriminate projected bananas from imagined bananas; thus the experiment involves distinguishing images from hallucinations, which is probably of little moment and not, at present, helpful. (Cf. Segal, Chapter 5, pp. 75-94.) Watson was content to assume that all reports of imagery were only matters of implicit verbalization or inner speech. Paivio (1967) has properly indicated that Watson's evidence here was just as inferential as might be the evidence for imagery.

Watson appears to have ignored commonly reported experiences which appear directly contradictory to the assumption that all imagery is inner speech, and which may throw some small light on our problem. There are three kinds of reports to consider: (1) People frequently report being unable to name someone or something quite familiar. The experience has been labeled "the tip of the tongue phenomenon (Brown and McNeill, 1966)." Supplying the name brings immediate recognition and relief. Presumably someone has been thinking about the unnamed person or object but could not verbalize the name. This might not prove that some other kind of activity, i.e., imagery, was taking place but there are plenty of reports of such activity. The forgetful person claims "I can see him plainly" but he cannot name him. (2) Another frequent report is of teachers or speakers saying one thing while thinking about another, especially of what is to be said next. Here again we find difficulty about accepting an overt speech exercise accompanying an implicit speech operation. "Thinking ahead" is usually reported in terms of some kind of visual imagery. (3) A third kind of conflict with the inner speech explanation can be observed in recall exercises when we are asked to name the members of a group of people or objects: old classmates, members of a team or family, a collection of animals, stamps, or anything not memorized as a verbal list. Here the typical report is of imagery preceding the occurrence of the name. I might recite the list of names of presidents of the United States in a verbal chain without much imagery, but the names of my nephews and nieces do not run off in the same fashion. Neither do the states of the United States. I "see" New Mexico next to Texas. These three types of phenomena do not provide evidence of anything, but do suggest researchable problems which might lead to a better account of imagery.

The situations just mentioned may help a little in providing some framework for an operational definition of our hypothetical construct. We see now, as one of the conditions for the emergence of imagery, the factor of failure of overt activity and even the absence of vocalization. Washburn's contribution here has already been cited. Her theory assumes that there may be blocking of overt motor activity. This may be due to conflict as in the 3 examples cited. But imagery may also emerge when there is inactivity even in the absence of conflict. Imagery and hallucinations play a prominent role in the allegedly mystical and ecstatic experiences of Yogis and Zen Buddhists which occur after long periods of immobilization. The common experience of dreaming while relatively immobile adds ready support to this hypothesis.

The argument that imagery is more prevalent in periods of overt inactivity has been developed recently by Fischer (1969, pp. 161–171) in a paper entitled "The perception-hallucination continuum." In this paper, contrary to Watson's emphasis on motoric explanations for dreams and imagery, Fischer propounds the view that imagery and hallucinations depend on a lack of movement or reduction thereof. We are all well acquainted with the sensory deprivation experiments where reports of hallucinatory experience were common. What we have failed to realize is that in those same experiments the subjects were relatively immobilized and were doing nothing with their bodies in any active sense of moving about or reacting to their environments. According to Zubek (1963) this simultaneous motor deprivation might be the real basis for the hallucinatory experiences, although subsequent researches by others have not been able to establish this conclusively.

Fischer exploits the apparent decline in motor activity when clinical or drugged patients are hallucinating into a theoretical conclusion that there is little or no imagery when a person is actively responding to his environment. When he is perceiving, he is engaged in reality testing, frequently by touching objects or making other responses to them as in stopping for a red traffic light. As motor activity drops off, e.g., in day dreaming, the amount of imaginal activity increases and with further decreases of such motor involvement, imagery becomes more and more prominent. Fischer is concerned with clinical cases with neurological damage or those under the influence of psychodysleptic drugs which inhibit motor activity chemically. The hallucinations of such cases, however, are not different in principle from various forms of imaging reported by people in normal circumstances. Dement (1965), in fact, ventures that the same mechanisms are responsible for hallucinations, images, and dreams, among other visionary experiences. The case for imaging made out by Hebb (1968) on the basis of phantom limb phenomena is another instance of the operation of imagery when there is no possibility of movement, even though Hebb's explanation is somewhat different.

Fischer calls attention to a feature of Rorschach analysis, first noted by Rorschach himself, that individuals achieving high scores on human movement *(M)* tended to be highly imaginative with inhibited motility. This suggestion is open to possible verification.

One of Fischer's own contributions is his development of a sensory-to-movement ratio. Subjects under the influence of psychodysleptic drugs indicate high ratios in their penmanship by showing little motor control and light pressure with large excursive writing compared to their normal hand. At the same time they are enjoying a hallucinatory, unrealistic evaluation of the writing they produce.

The recent research on dreams offers some promise, although again the data here are subject to Watsonian criticism. Watson had no trouble with dreams. People just talked to themselves while asleep, some quite vocally, others implicitly. Watson seized with alacrity upon the research on the dreams of the deaf. The finger movements of deaf dreamers were precisely what he needed. The current emphasis on REM activity in dreams would only add peripheral activity to any implicit verbal activity and support Watson's views.

The fact that eye movements occur during dreaming might have added strength to Watson's peripheral interpretation of imagery. Recent studies by Graham (1970), however, indicate that the eye movements displayed by *S*s who are trying to "image" something in motion, e.g., a pendulum, are not the same as those in actually observing the object. There are movements, to be sure, but they are quantitatively and qualitatively different. The interpretation of these studies is difficult. The imagery may not have been of good quality because the movements were not precise or there may be additional features to an image besides the eye movements.

There is, however, a notable feature of dream behavior, first noted by Dement (1965), which might have given Watson pause. During periods of REM with presumed strong likelihood of dreaming, the body activity is strikingly reduced or inhibited. This curious inhibition of the body during dreams may be one of the prerequisities for effective imagery. The relative absence of bodily movement when imagery (or dreaming, in this instance) has been reported has long been known according to introspective accounts. The old introspectionists identified the presence of imagery with a suspension of external activity or, at best, subdued motoric outlets.

Thus, regardless of how we interpret the data from dreams and drugs, there appears to be at least one identifying feature of imagery that may lead to a closer analysis namely, the lack of movement of the gross musculature! This finding may in part explain some negative reports of individuals who claim they have no imagery. They may be somewhat hyperkinetic types, restless, twitchy, or otherwise motorically engaged.

In the early history of psychology we read accounts of the difficulty of training effective introspectors. Such difficulty may have occurred because while the introspectionist is actively engaged in reporting on his imagery there would be little prospect for imagery to operate.

Any activity of the body is likely to interfere with imagery and prevent it; even trying to have an image may well stop such processes and this may explain why Watson (also William James, 1890, and Wundt, 1929, by their own admissions) had none. Every time he deliberately tried to have an image he would fail. It is probably impossible to have an image of any specific kind if it is somehow personally ordered. (For contrasting views, cf. Barber, Segal, and Paivo, Chapters 6, 5, and 2.) When I look at a particular book, shut my eyes and try to image it, I invariably fail. The same book can be imaged without great difficulty when some other circumstance calls for it.

Here we may have another feature of imagery: it cannot be dictated or directed by the imager. Images are involuntary occurrences, subject to no one's personal control. Even when someone else suggests the desired images, they may not emerge or occur. In my studies of mediation I have tried to propose possible associative imagery by which a pair of nonsense syllables or words might be remembered. The subjects frequently object and find their own mediators. They do not find them by looking for them, however; they occur and are accepted or found unlikely and rejected.

Thus far, our attempt to anchor the construct of the image at both ends appears to be failing at both ends. We cannot specify the stimulus with precison nor can we specify the response. Leuba's conditioning procedure might help remedy the former weakness, but it again demonstrates the involuntary nature of the image. It is proper to note here that Leuba's hypnosis procedure also called for relaxation or relative immobility. We seem to have arrived at a situation where we can say that an image is something that happens to us when we are relatively quiet, not talking, or unable to talk, and not trying to have images. The implication here is that we are in a condition beyond or outside of or without sensory control. When there is direct sensory control we can respond effectively by one form of action or another, including speech. When there is less immediate motor adjustment, images occur whether we are asleep or awake. The suggestion is obvious that when our brains have nothing to do for us, they work for themselves, and that images are the operations of relatively independent action of our brains, or in Hebb's terms, spontaneous neural discharges. Because there is usually a modicum of sensory input, the resultant imagery is not a haywire brainstorm, but is reasonably orderly.

Thus far our knowledge of the neurology of imagery is meager. There is no known localization. Although Penfield (1951) obtained imagery by electrical stimulation of the temporal lobe, he concluded that the sites of stimulation could not be identified as the loci of imagery. Stimulation by implants, where attempted, has not established any imagery areas.

The postulation of a neural mechanism for imagery does not solve the problem. Such reductionism avoids the problem by passing it on to physiologists while the psychologists use hypothetical constructs freely, or, as in the case of Skinner, ignore the internal or implicit reactions of the organism on the grounds of disinterest. There are other objections to physiological (materialist) reductionism, but they are largely philosophical in nature, pertaining to concepts of causality which need not concern us here.

However, such an approach does make it palatable to recognize that images are activations of some physical structures; they are not things in themselves, but rather, they are processes, neural activities of real protoplasm in a real body. While no solution to the problem, such an inference provides new prospects. It suggests that images are not static pictures but are processes that begin and end with varying existences. Here again research prospects emerge: when certain neural elements are operative and these are followed by others, the two neural processes can come to operate together either simultaneously, in sequence, or in a circular fashion. On future occasions either process could excite the other.

A clear case can be made out for such a proposal. In my use of the mnemonic technique of rhymes and numerals (Bugelski, Kidd, and Segman, 1968; Bugelski, 1968) subjects are taught a rhyme associating each number with a concrete concept ("one is a bun, two is a shoe"). When trying to learn 10 new words, the subjects peg each word to the concept appropriate to its ordinal position through a mediating image. On inquiry, my subjects have no problem providing either the number or the object presumably associated with the number. Here, there is a striking contrast to ordinary nonsense syllable or verbal learning, where such "backward" learning is normally difficult to demonstrate. Here we also have a potential account of "clustering" phenomena. When a list with words of several categories is read to subjects, they will, in general, tend to recall category items together even if they had been separated in the list. All that needs be assumed is that traces of each stimulus word are still active when other words of the category are read or that they are reactivated by the new words because of frequent associations in the past. In the recall, such tendencies to activate each other are presumably aroused, and the subject responds by categories. He does no subjective organizing by himself. It all happens to him or for him.

In a preliminary effort at supporting this view I had some 20 college students view 16 small cartoons of common objects such as spoons, automobiles, dogs, pencils, and balls, as they were exposed, apparently at random, on a board where they were mounted in a 4 × 4 matrix.[3] The Ss were then asked to face another board with 16 blank square cards facing them and recall the location of as many items as they could. One half of the Ss were instructed to form associated images as each picture was shown. The other group was simply instructed to try to remember the locations. The recall scores were not different (11.2 and 10.7) so far as accuracy was concerned. I was interested in the order of the recall, however, and compared the recall of each card with its exposure order. The experimental Ss recalled 6.9 cards in the order of presentation. The control Ss recalled only 1.9 sequences. The control Ss tried to use other strategies such as left-to-right, row and column, and tried to rebuild the 4 × 4 square in an orderly fashion. The experimental Ss were guided by the associations formed during the exposure period. About half of the sequential associations were in a "backward" order, thus if "auto" followed "spoon" in the original presentation, the S might reverse this order in recall and say "auto, spoon." In the original presentation (5 seconds per picture) the Ss commonly glanced back and forth between the pictures just shown and their predecessors; such a pattern of inspection would readily provide for a seemingly backward sequence in reporting.

My original reason for embarking on this study was to test the hypothesis that images are not static processes that can be held or controlled by a subject but that there is a dynamic feature to imagery which results in one image quickly giving way to another. The old introspectionists referred to this as the fleeting quality of imagery. They are not so much fleeting as changing, one calling up another. A rapid sequence would probably result in a kaleidoscopic effect which would cancel out any effective reaction. The S could then talk about "blurring," "lack of clarity," and "instability." Such reports would indicate not a lack of imagery but an embarrassment of riches. It would be the equivalent of what Hebb (1949) referred to as t, a complex activation of many cell assembly components giving rise to some kind of general reaction which would have no specific features because it had too many such specific units. It would be, in effect, a concept.

[3] I am indebted to Carol McMahon for conducting this experiment.

Perhaps we have made a little progress. Work with the young deaf, the aphasics, and further efforts such as those of the Gardners (1969) to teach their chimpanzee, Washoe, to use the sign language of the deaf may help. Washoe makes the sign for "dog" when she hears a bark. Presumably she somehow knew about the source of a bark before she learned to sign "dog." If a chimpanzee can make a series of signs that communicate something about absent stimuli and makes these signs systematically at appropriate occasions, we must assume (as with the "tip of the tongue phenomenon") that she has something to talk about. That something is presumably an image.

We come now to the experimental situations where investigators attempt to have subjects experience imagery. The instructions will refer to pictures, imagination, or thoughts. Subjects will normally accede, and report imagery in varying, though frequently copious, amounts. The suggestion emerges that an operational definition can be generated from the the instructional and response features to the effect that when subjects are instructed to form images, and subsequently display a difference in behavior from subjects otherwise treated identically except for references to imagery, then the differences in the results are due to imagery. It is difficult to give such a definition credence and respect because of its obvious circularity. Reports of images are still only reports, not images. What is important is to include appropriate controls for verbalization in the instructions given to control subjects. When this is done to the best of our capability, we may still not have isolated imagery functions, but only have excluded certain kinds of specifically controlled verbalization operations. In my work with a mnemonic scheme, subjects reported a great deal of detail about the nature of the things they were imagining when they had been asked to associate the words via imagery. When they were asked to learn the same words in sentences, they had no such detailed reports. Instructions to image may just generate more verbalization than instructions to verbalize in these circumstances.

The experimental design that might establish the reality and function of imagery on a scientific basis appears to be the same as for any other phenomenon, namely, the institution of the proper controls. If we wish to demonstrate the operation of imagery in a given situation, we must test the dependent variable when no imagery is feasible. If a verbal variable could be the real factor, the verbal variable should also be varied systematically. Differences in the imagery and nonimagery condition will reveal the degree of the imagery effect. Differences in the verbal and nonverbal conditions can likewise be compared. In this way we approach a crucial experiment. But how are we to exclude imagery while permitting verbal behavior?

An attempt to exclude imagery in a verbal (PA) learning situation was made by Morelli (1970). He compared Ss learning under three conditions: with pictures of stimulus word objects, with nonsense diagrams over the stimulus words, and words alone. With this procedure he hoped to interfere with the imagery that might normally be aroused by the stimulus words. He found that the picture groups and verbal groups did not differ. From this he came to the untestable conclusion that both groups used imagery. The nonsense picture group did significantly worse. Does this prove that the assumed imagery was being interfered with by the nonsense picture? While possible, such a conclusion is only tentative, as it might simply be a matter of distraction from the learning task. The Ss might easily have been under the impression that the nonsense figures were in some way relevant and should be attended to. Their task was clearly a more difficult one.

This brings us back to the problem of proper design. An obvious experimental design is to select either blind or deaf subjects and submit them to situations in which visual or auditory imagery can be assumed to be missing but where language capacity can be observed.[4] Working on this assumption, I presumed that blind people should have greater difficulty with words that refer to strictly visual phenomena, whereas the deaf would have trouble with words of a purely auditory character. I proceeded to make up a list of 8 "auditory" words such as echo, thunder, and music; 8 "visual" words such as lightning, shadow, mirror, and red; and 8 "neutral" words such as table, shoe, and hair. Armed with this list I asked 28 blind children (11–19 years) and a similar age group of deaf children (N=107) to learn these words as response associates to a list of 24 neutral words such as apple and stove.[5] The same words were learned by a group of 15 nonhandicapped girls (ages 17–19). The results followed the same pattern in all of the groups. The neutral words were easiest (perhaps due to multiple imagery), then came the visual words, finally the auditory words. The words were obviously not equated for difficulty, but I was looking for differences in ratios of recall. The results are shown

TABLE 1
Percent Correct Recall of Neutral, Visual, and Auditory Words[a]

	Eight neutral words	Eight visual words	Eight auditory words
Normal	83.3	79.1	75.0
Blind	67.4	63.9	61.8
Deaf	57.2	53.31	39.85

[a]Among normal, blind, and deaf (children) after 1 trial learning of 24 words.

in Tables 1 and 2. The differences might be subject to some discussion but they really throw no light on the imagery problem. It is clear that these auditory words are difficult for all groups. While the deaf sample has the most trouble with the auditory words, there is a possible confounding because deaf children will not be

[4] The entire field of aphasia where language may be ineffective but where imagery might be functional also deserves intensive study.

[5] Sandra Lattanzio assisted me in conducting these studies.

TABLE 2

Percent Recall of Visual, Auditory, and Neutral Words by Blind
and Deaf Children

Words	Blind children[a]	Deaf children[a]
Visual		
Picture	44.4	37.6
Lightning	50.0	31.6
Cloud	50.0	47.9
Shadow	61.1	32.5
Negro	72.2	59.8
Fog	77.8	62.4
Red	77.8	78.6
Blue	77.8	76.1
Auditory		
Whistle	50.0	43.6
Bark	50.0	42.7
Whisper	55.5	20.5
Squeak	61.1	33.3
Music	66.7	52.1
Crackle	66.7	34.2
Echo	66.7	43.6
Thunder	77.8	48.7
Neutral		
Glove	44.4	35.9
Key	50.0	46.2
Airplane	55.5	63.2
Rope	61.1	41.0
Truck	66.7	31.6
Sofa	72.2	70.1
Hair	88.9	73.5
Shoe	100.0	95.7

[a]Percent correct (18 Ss).

taught auditory words with any great enthusiasm in the first place and such words would certainly be relatively unfamiliar. What puzzled me most was why the blind youths learned the visual words better than the auditory ones. This seemed so improper and uncooperative of them. Further analysis of the data, however, provided an answer. It appears that every word that I used had a different meaning for the blind children, and they used that meaning instead of the one I had intended. The blind Ss simply translated visual words into nonvisual ones, for example: lightning became *fast,* blue became *unhappy,* shadow became *to follow,* fog became *lost,* red became a *party* or *Santa Claus.* For *cloud* and *picture,* however, translations were not available so readily and only a few of the Ss learned these words. Similarly, the deaf Ss were able to translate *music* into *dancing, bark* into *dog,* and thereby gain some success. Again, only a few could handle *whisper.* It should be quite obvious that nobody whispers to the deaf and for any of them to learn such a word is somewhat astonishing.

But my biggest obstacle was the subjects themselves. They were not completely blind or deaf. They were legally blind or hard of hearing but none of them was an ideal *S,* purely and thoroughly, and was not congenitally blind or deaf. Without such ideal *S*s, the experiment cannot be interpreted with confidence. At the Buffalo Association for the Blind, I was able to find a 21-year-old man who was totally and congenitally blind. He was pleased to serve as a subject along with 9 other legally (not congenitally) blind *S*s in a simple learning experiment wherein I used the one-bun mnemonic scheme. All *S*s learned 3 lists in separate sessions, a week apart, in random order. The first list consisted of neutral words, the second of color terms, and the third of what I have called "visual" words (see Table 3).

The results of interest were that the 9 legally blind *S*s learned all 3 lists without significant differences, but my congenitally blind *S* had undue trouble learning the 10 color associates. He required 15 trials to learn the color list and only 3 trials and 1 trial, respectively, for the other 2 lists. The so-called "visual words" were remembered in 1 trial. Only one other *S* had any trouble with the color words (10 trials) but this *S* also had trouble with the other lists and could be considered a slow learner. Having exhausted my supply of congenitally blind and available *S*s I must temporarily rest my case on my one *S* who could not learn the color associates.

Assuming his data to be true indicants of some general trend, it appears that words that cannot excite any visual reaction, and consequently cannot be the basis for imagery, leave *S* without a foundation for learning. Such words are true

TABLE 3

Trials to Learn and Number of Words Correct on the First Trial[a]

Subject	Neutral words		Color words		Visual words	
	Trials	First trial	Trials	First trial	Trials	First trial
1	7	1	4	1	5	2
2	1	10	1	10	2	8
3	3	7	15	5	1	10
4	2	8	3	4	3	6
5	2	8	1	10	1	10
6	6	1	10	3	8	2
7	7	2	3	6	4	4
8	3	7	2	9	2	8
9	4	5	5	3	4	4
10	3	7	2	8	2	8

[a]For 10 blind *S*s in a paired-associate task with different response terms to mnemonic stimulus words.

nonsense syllables for such *S*s. They are learned differently from other, more meaningful words which do have a sensory base in some prior experience.

At this point it is valuable to try to come to terms with words which elicit little or no imagery in normal persons. Words which elicit little imagery are generally abstract; Paivio, Yuille, and Madigan (1968) found that concreteness and imagery were highly correlated in the norms they developed. A close examination of Paivio's norms, however, suggests interesting points concerning how words come to arouse imagery.

All words are abstract to begin with. As physical stimuli, written or spoken, they can be described in some kinds of physical terms, but it is quite clear that each word employed or heard is a learned response with its own history. It may be that the imagery ratings can in some way be related to past experiences with the word as a response. A word like "cat" is usually considered "concrete," because it refers to a specific instance, while "animal" is regarded as more abstract by some writers in linguistics. Paivio's norms (1968) show "cat" as rating 7.00 and "animal" as 6.75—not much of a distinction on a 7-point scale. A child whose own cat is named "Kitty" could not rate Kitty, a specific name applied to a specific cat, as any more "concrete" than 7.00, yet *cat* can very well be considered logically a class term covering a wide variety of kinds of cats: Manx, Siamese, Maltese, Calico, Persian, Domestic Shorthair, wild, alley, house, etc. The word feline might be thought of as more abstract (Paivio's sample rate it at 5.31) but it is only a synonym for most students, and a low-frequency one at that. Perhaps abstract words are only low-frequency synonyms. Of the 3 terms, "Kitty," "cat," and "feline," only "Kitty" should be described as concrete in the sense of a specific, real world, detonation. "Cat" is connotative, even though one can point to a representative of the species. For the child beginning to learn, the question "Is that a cat, too?" can only be asked after a first cat is labeled and a second one appears.

A perusal of Paivio's list raises some rather interesting points in that a number of words that are considered to be rather abstract class terms by logicians or lexicographers are given high ratings for concreteness and imagery. Among these are the examples given in Table 4.

It seems that words encompass a multitude of individual representations or even subclasses. When such words as *circle* and *square* achieve high ratings for imagery and concreteness, this probably indicates that the words were *not* being responded to as class labels but in terms of specific instances. The lack of a distinction in the ratings of *house* and *home* may have obtained because the raters thought of a specific house which was also the home. Likewise, it seems plausible that the reason *S*s gave high ratings to "animal" (6.75) and "vegetable" (6.76) is that they were responding to some specific instance such as cat (7.00) or corn (6.90) instead of the class label.

The question that now arises is the logical one of whether anyone ever responds to a class label per se, or always responds with a specific instance, along

TABLE 4
Ratings for Some Sample Words from Paivio's List[a]

	I	C	m	F
Animal	6.10	6.75	2.70	AA
Appliance	5.73	6.45	6.64	7
Camouflage	5.20	5.26	6.38	2
Cash	6.17	6.28	7.21	46
Circle	6.23	6.00	4.88	AA
Colony	5.10	5.87	5.00	A
Green	6.60	5.46	6.08	AA
Fowl	5.87	6.58	7.36	20
Home	6.50	6.25	6.08	AA
House	6.67	6.93	6.83	AA
Insect	6.10	6.80	6.32	40
Instrument	5.67	6.25	6.72	42
Square	6.37	5.70	5.44	AA
Vegetable	5.83	6.76	6.92	A

[a]Imagery (I), concreteness (C), meaningfulness (m), and Thorndike-Lorge frequency (F).

the lines of Berkeley's famous argument that he always thought of a specific horse and not of horses in general when that term was introduced. Note now that Berkeley does not consider the word "horse" as a concrete word, though virtually all of Paivio's subjects do (6.94). The word *horse*, like most nouns (except specific proper names or unique objects, e.g., the sun), is a class label and thereby qualifies as a philosopher's abstraction or "idea." For the psychologist, however, it may well be that words like table, cat, corn, or horse are responded to as concrete because people, unlike philosophers, respond in terms of their own specific and individual experiences to any word. If they rate a word as abstract, it is because they have less familiarity (frequency of experience) with it, as for example, "forethought" (1.83). A word may also be *identified* as abstract by some rule learned in grammar school about abstract versus concrete words, e.g., "collective nouns," or names of activities (politics, football, democracy) or words that stem from verb or adjective bases, but have been transformed into nouns by suffixes (kiss, kindness).

An abstract *term* is based on translation from concrete instances. Some abstract terms are purely abstract in that they have only verbal substitutes (synonyms) as referents. They are the pure symbols, such as numerals or formulas in mathematics, completely new words which have never been heard before, or words in a strange, foreign language.

The word "imagery" is itself an abstract term and does not conjure up an image in the hearer other than, perhaps, some inappropriate reference to screens or pictures. One could utter a complete sentence, e.g., "An image is a conditioned sensation" without arousing imagery. The question then follows: Does this sentence have any meaning without imagery? One can say he understands the sentence and therefore it must have meaning, but what that means, in turn, is that at one time he must have had imagery related to specific instances of images, conditioning, and sensations. After many such experiences, the words themselves have come to operate quite independently of imagery, appropriate reactions occur in a listener, and a conversation can proceed on a verbal level with little or no imagery. The people are then speaking abstractly. The imagery, if any, might be verbal or auditory; i.e., of the words themselves, what James called "verbal imagery."

We might illustrate with reference to numbers. A numeral like 7 can evoke an image of the number itself. This image has specific characteristics, hence a European 7 with a slash through it looks odd to Americans—just as the absence of the slash must look odd to Europeans. But there is no necessity for such an image if we are dealing simply with numbers and not "seven sons" or "seven seas," or "seven ages." The number has been used in so many contexts of seven objects, that no specific image needs be aroused. It can be reacted to on its own abstract level, as an odd number, as an item to be added or multiplied, etc. It is a learned response made to certain stimuli and we can say we know what it means without reference to concrete or specific objects.

It frequently happens in any language that some word will acquire usage as a substitute for a prior, commonly used word, and no longer call forth the imagery that gave meaning to the earlier word; e.g., you learn to say *viscera* instead of *guts*. *Emotion* becomes *affective process* or *affect* and loses affect in the process. Drives become motivation, and motivation becomes conation, and we no longer have images of hungry rats. *Slums* become the *inner city* or the *core area*. The *poor* become *underprivileged* or *culturally deprived*.

What happens then with abstract words is that they serve some conversational purpose at some level that usually delays genuine communication. Nothing much is going to be done for the "culturally deprived." Something might be done for the residents of a "slum." A campaign for "rodent control" might not do as much as a "kill the rats" proposal, and if we talked about the "scum on the river" we might get more action than if we talk about "pollution."

The use of abstract words is a higher or second order of operation. At first, especially with children, translation into concrete instances is required. A child told not to be a nuisance must first ask, "What's a nuisance?" When this is translated for him as, "Don't bother me when I'm busy," he may be satisfied if he can readily translate "bother" and "busy" into concrete imagery. After further experience with "nuisance" he begins to use and misuse the term in broader and broader circumstances so that it no longer elicits the early imagery that gave it a somewhat precise meaning.

On a different level of abstraction we must consider other grammatical constructions like conjunctions, prepositions, and modifiers like adjectives and adverbs, as well as pronouns and even verbs. Paivio used only nouns, it should be noted. There are other kinds of words, however, where imagery is at least alleged to be meager if not entirely missing. Words such as *and, but, under, it, the* have no meaning. Sentences containing only such words are meaningless. If we say we understand these words or that they do have meaning, we find that we cannot provide explanations of such words without reference to nouns. When Edmund Burke Huey (1908) tried to explain reading as a matter of image arousal, he hesitated at drawing the conclusion because there are no images for many words, especially non-noun words such as *or, the, but,* or *under.* He cites Titchener's problems with finding an image for "but" which Titchener finally described as the image of the rear of a man's head. The man was a colleague who frequently used "but" when speaking on a platform where Titchener sat behind him. Titchener should not have tried so hard. We might not be too successful with "but" either, but consider prepositions for a moment. A preposition cannot have meaning in and of itself. It always describes a so-called relationship between at least two things. A book is *on* a table. There is no difficulty with imagery in this case. Anyone can imagine a book and a table and the book on the surface of the table. There is no need to image "on" as a separate act. Similarly for any other preposition, there is always more than one item to image with another. The man *on* the horse, the dog *with* the cat, etc.

Verbs by themselves, without agents, again are meaningless. If we are forced to deal with a pure verb, e.g., "fight," we quickly supply an agent and an object if necessary, because transitive verbs not only take an object, but virtually require one. A statement like *men fight* is incomplete and we will not leave it in that state. We will automatically provide objects in our imaginal reactions. Men fight among themselves, against obstacles or enemies, for causes, etc. The causes then conjure up their own images.

There appears to me good reason to accept Paivio's (1970) assertion that aroused imagery may explain more than the so-called "deep-structure" of the linguists. (Also discussed by Paivio in Chapter 2, pp. 7–32.) With low imagery components or high levels of abstraction we could expect difficulty in learning or communication because there would be a need for translation, not by transformational grammar, but into substitute terminology with some more effective and less elusive imagery.

However, we must not be too quick in downgrading words while upgrading imagery, or we shall find ourselves with nothing to talk with. We cannot afford to do what Watson did in reverse; that is, throw out language and retain imagery as our basic tool of thinking and meaning. Words have their own role. At levels of operation which are marked by high frequency usage, high concreteness, and high imagery value, the probability is that imagery is of the greatest importance in behavior. Such behavior is probably common to man, chimpanzees, and cats. At higher levels of abstraction or low imagery, words function in their own right as symbols, and can be used for certain functions where concrete and specific instances cannot be anticipated. The typical instance is the legal use of words, the definitions of crimes; e.g., obscenity or fraud.

Mathematicians and natural scientists, similarly, can use words or pictographic symbols and operate on these without any reference to words denoting concrete objects. Einstein's $E = mc^2$ or Galileo's $S = \frac{1}{2}gt^2$ lend themselves to purely verbal (i.e., logical) or other symbolic manipulation without any need, use, or likelihood of imagery. Any imagery involved is likely to be worthless or even negative as in the case of $F = MA$.

Words, then, need no defense. Imagery too needs no defense. They both need to be put into their appropriate places.

In summary, I have tried to approach the problem of defining the image by describing the conditions under which imagery might best be experimentally investigated. While I have emphasized relative immobility of the gross musculature, I have not excluded more modest peripheral activity. Again, while I have emphasized central neural discharges, I have not excluded either external (conditioned) stimuli, nor, at least incipient motor outlets. I have tried to emphasize the point that imagery is an active process and not a thing in the sense of an object. If we think in terms of a verb instead of a noun, we will have made some progress. Perhaps we could reduce the frequency of usage of such terms as "image" and "imagery" while we raise the frequency of "imaging."

REFERENCES

Brown, R., & McNeill, D. "The tip of the tongue phenomenon." *Journal of Verbal Learning and Verbal Behavior,* 1966, **5,** 325-337.

Bugelski, B. R. Images as mediators in one-trial paired-associate learning. *Journal of Experimental Psychology,* 1968, **77,** 328-334.

Bugelski, B. R., Kidd, E., & Segman, S. The image as a mediator in one-trial paired-associate learning. *Journal of Experimental Psychology,* 1968, **76,** 69-73.

Dement, W. C. An essay on dreams. The role of physiology in understanding their nature. In *New Directions in Psychology II.* New York: Holt, Rinehart, and Winston, 1965.

Farber, I. E. Personality and behavior science. In Brodbeck, M. (Ed.), *Readings in the Philosophy of the Social Sciences.* New York: Macmillan, 1968.

Fischer, R. The perception-hallucination continuum. *Diseases of the nervous system,* 1969, **30,** 161-171.

Gardner, R. A., & Gardner, B. T. Teaching sign language to a chimpanzee. *Science,* 1969, **165,** 664-672.

Graham, K. R. Eye movements during visual mental imagery. Paper presented at the 41st annual meeting of the Eastern Psychological Association, April, 1970.

Hebb, D. O. *The organization of behavior.* New York: Wiley, 1949.

Hebb, D. O. Concerning imagery. *Psychological Review,* 1968, **75,** 466-477.

Horowitz, M. Psychic trauma. *Archives of general psychiatry,* 1969, **20,** 552-557.

Huey, E. B. *The psychology and pedagogy of reading.* New York: Macmillan, 1908. (Reprinted 1968 by M.I.T. Press, Cambridge, Mass.)

James, W. *The principles of psychology.* New York: Holt, 1890.

Klüver, H. Eidetic phenomena. *Psychological Bulletin,* 1932, **29,** 181-203.

Kotarbinski, T. *Gnosiology.* New York: Pergamon Press, 1966.

Koch, S. Clark L. Hull. In William Estes *et al.* (Eds.), *Modern Learning Theory.* New York: Appleton, 1954.

Leuba, C. Images as conditioned sensations. *Journal of Experimental Psychology,* 1940, **26,** 345-351.

Miller, G. A., Galanter, E., & Pribram, K. H. *Plans and the structure of behavior.* New York: Holt, 1960.

Morelli, G. Pictures and competing pictures as mediators in paired-associate learning. *Perceptual and motor skills,* 1970, **30,** 729-730.

Mowrer, O. H. *Learning theory and the symbolic processes.* New York: Wiley, 1960.

Paivio, A. Meaning, mediation, and memory. *Research Bulletin No. 48.* Department of Psychology, London, Ontario, Canada: The University of Western Ontario, 1967.

Paivio, A. Mental imagery in associative learning and memory. *Psychological Review,* 1969, **76,** 241-263.

Paivio, A. Imagery and natural language. Symposium address. American Educational Research Association Meeting. Minneapolis, March 6, 1970.

Paivio, A., Yuille, C., & Madigan, S. A. Concreteness, imagery, and meaningfulness values for 925 nouns. *Journal of Experimental Psychology Monograph Supplement.* 1968, **76,** No. 1, Part 2.

Penfield, W. Memory mechanisms. *Transactions of the American Neurological Association.* 1951, **76,** 15-31.

Perky, C. W. Experimental study of imagination. *American Journal of Psychology,* 1910, **21,** 422-452.

Richardson, A. *Mental imagery,* New York: Springer, 1969.

Titchener, E. B. *Textbook of psychology.* New York: The Macmillan Co., 1921.

Tulving, E. Subjective organization in free recall of "unrelated words." *Psychological Review,* 1962, **69,** 344-354.

Washburn, M. F. *Movement and mental imagery.* New York: Houghton Mifflin, 1916.

Watson, J. B. Psychology as the behaviorist views it. *Psychological Review,* 1913, **20,** 158-177.

Watson, J. B. *Behaviorism.* New York: W. W. Norton, 1924.

Watson, J. B. *The ways of behaviorism.* New York: Harper & Brothers, 1928.

Wundt, W., see Boring, E. G. *A history of experimental psychology.* New York: Appleton-Century, 1929.

Zubek, J. P., Aftanas, M., Kovach, K., Wilgosh, L., & Winocur, G. The effect of severe immobilization of the body on intellectual and perceptual processes. *Canadian Journal of Psychology,* 1963, **17,** 118-133.

CHAPTER 5

PROCESSING OF THE STIMULUS IN IMAGERY AND PERCEPTION

Sydney Joelson Segal[1]

The question of the distinction between imagery and perception is so old that it may seem that only the antiquarians are interested in tracing whether Aristotle should be credited with first considering images to be revivifications of former sensations, or if Hume is responsible for the assumption during the last several centuries that images are paler replicas of previously experienced percepts. Considerable time and effort was spent in the early psychological laboratories pursuing this problem; possible quantitative differences between the image and the percept were explored in Wundt's laboratory by Scripture, Külpe, and others, and Titchener set up his own laboratory and tried to demonstrate that the answer lay in qualitative differences instead. A considerable body of research by Titchener and his students was directed to this aim, but the aim and the entire introspectionist approach was seriously questioned by the experimental work of C. W. Perky (1910), a student in Titchener's own laboratory.

Perky devised a special experimental method in which observers looked at a small spot in the center of a window, and were instructed to imagine different items at that spot. Unknown to them, faintly colored replicas of the items imaged,

[1] This report was prepared and much of the reported research carried out under AFOSR contract F-44620-68C-0093. I gratefully acknowledge the helpful advice of Jerome L. Singer, Robert R. Holt, and Gertrude Schmeidler in preparing this manuscript.

fluctuating in intensity and oscillating slightly, were projected from behind the window around the spot. The subjects continued to describe their imagery; and, although they reported images which often resembled the stimulus so closely that they seemed to be describing the projection, most of them continued firmly to believe that everything they described was a product of their own imagination.

Thus Perky's study seemed to suggest that trained introspectionists could not differentiate their images from perceptions. Neither Titchener nor Wundt could accept such an interpretation; it was readily rejected, even though it accorded with the earlier findings of Külpe; Titchener had other students who failed to replicate Perky's results and the issue was dropped. The accession of Watson a few years later swept the problem off the main stage of psychology. The behaviorists questioned whether a human observer could even legitimately report on a percept: hence, how could he possibly give a reliable verbal report of an image?

Today, however, as it is again possible to discuss imagery seriously (Hebb, 1968; Neisser, 1970), it may be well to evaluate these old questions once again. In what ways do the percept and the image differ? How can one distinguish them as a human observer? Is there a basic distinction in the processes involved in the two experiences? In this chapter I will review some of the literature which bears on this question, and also report on some of the results in my own replications of Perky's experiment.

Sometimes a perception is defined as an experience occurring in response to a physical stimulus, but an image or hallucination is defined as a qualitatively similar subjective experience which occurs when there is no physical stimulus. In the present discussion, however, these definitions will be set aside to try to arrive at an empirically derived analysis of the nature of perception and imagery, and their relationship to the physical "stimulus."

Attempts to compare imagery to perception have frequently focused on the most extreme situations. If an image is the same as a perception, then it should show aftereffects, Mach bands, illusions, and so on. Many turn-of-the-century psychologists assumed that if an image was a weaker replica of a perception, it should be possible to reinstate a total perceptual experience through imagery.

AFTERIMAGES FROM IMAGED COLORS

Many researchers have believed that hypnotized subjects could be induced to perform astounding feats. Could they mimic a perceptual experience under hypnosis also? Binet and Féré (1891), writing on mesmerism, revealed a variety of situations in which hypnotized subjects were able to reinstate a perceptual-like experience. They described many anecdotal instances, and also reported some experimental data. In one task, previously described by Wundt, the subject hallucinated a colored form, and then reported subsequent afterimages. Binet and Féré directed subjects to "hallucinate" a red square on a sheet of white paper; when a fresh sheet of white paper was placed before them, subjects reported "seeing" a green square.

These findings have been repeated frequently. In a complex design in which colors were imaged under hypnosis and subjects immediately awakened and asked to report on afterimages, Hibler (1938) obtained essentially negative results. He asserted that positive findings were probably due to suggestion. Rosenthal and Mele (1952), however, reported positive results with 4 subjects; 3 of them had had no previous knowledge of afterimages and the fourth had partly erroneous knowledge, yet all reported afterimages. Therefore, Rosenthal and Mele asserted that suggestion played a minor role. Erickson and Erickson (1938) reported positive findings with 4 out of 5 subjects; the fifth was unable to hallucinate the primary color.

Barber (1959, 1964) reviewed the findings on this topic and concluded that the results were equivocal. In his own experiments, he found that only 2 out of 6 hypnotized subjects were able to hallucinate the color blue within a pencilled circle; these 2 subjects were also able to hallucinate other colors, and had negative afterimages to all. All 6 subjects were given posthypnotic amnesia and the same procedure was followed in the waking state. Again, only 2 subjects were able to image the primary colors, and both described afterimages; these were not the same 2 subjects who showed the effect under hypnosis. The findings with imagery were replicated with a sample of 11 subjects; only 2 were able to image the primary color, but both reported afterimages. More recently, Barber (Chapter 6, pp. 118-120) questioned even some of these findings.

In 1901 Downey found one subject who could image colors readily and who obtained afterimages quite consistently without hypnosis. Perky (1910) also had noted that some of her subjects' images were followed by negative afterimages. Külpe (1902) reported that some of his sophisticated subjects tried to use the presence of afterimages as a clue that a given experience had been "objective" in origin, but this clue led to erroneous "false alarms" as often as it led to correct judgments; thus for his subjects there were no reliable differences between the afterimages of an imaged (or partly imaged) experience and the afterimages of an objective occurrence.

While Barber concluded that suggestion played a major role in the positive findings, this may not be the whole explanation. Stromeyer (1970) in studying an extreme eidetic subject (described more fully below), reported that she developed an afterimage to a colored display. The eidetic afterimage was not identical to a true afterimage—for example, it did not follow Emmert's law—but neither was it a product of suggestion.

On the other hand, if one instructs an imaging subject—whether hypnotized or not—to suppress perception of a color, the afterimage to the color is generally *not* suppressed. Thus a subject might—under suggestion or hypnosis—report that a red square looked gray and colorless, but it still generated a green afterimage (Binet and Féré, 1891). Likewise, it is difficult to reproduce all the responses of normal color-blindness (Binet and Féré, 1891). Miller, Lundy, and Galbraith (1969) instructed 10 hypnotized subjects to hallucinate a red filter. While all reported the apparent color change in a visual display, none of them were able to see numbers in the display which were immediately visible when they donned a pair of spectacles with real red filters.

IMAGING ILLUSIONS AND OTHER SENSORY PHENOMENA

Attempts to induce an illusion by asking subjects to image the inducing background around a real test figure, or vice versa, are sometimes successful (Underwood, 1960; Malhotra, 1958; Singer and Sheehan, 1965); but subjects were never able to "blot out" a real inducing background and see an undistorted test figure (Underwood, 1960). Crovitz (1969) reported on his effort to instruct subjects to imagine the pulsing light that determines the CFF. First, using a slow rate, he asked subjects to regard the pulsing light, then he removed the stimulus and asked them to image it. Subjects could not report a satisfactory image of a light flashing faster than about 5 cps, although their CFF to the real light was as fast as 45 cps.

It seems that the image rarely can mimic effects that depend on unique properties of the peripheral sense organs. Nevertheless, there are occasional exceptions even to this rule. Thus Binet and Féré (1891) reported that pupillary diameter accommodates according to the assumed distance of an object imagined under hypnosis. Luria, (1968) reporting on a mnemonist with primitive and uniquely vivid imagery, found his subject able to dark adapt his eyes by imagery, to evidence a cochlear-pupil reflex by imagining a sound, and to suppress alpha rhythms by imaging a bright light.

The imagery reported by Luria's mnemonist was so vivid that he frequently could not distinguish it from a percept. "I'd look at a clock and for a long while continue to see the hands fixed just as they were, and not realize time has passed . . . (Luria, 1968, p. 152)."

EIDETIC IMAGERY

Luria's mnemonist and also Downey's subject may have been eidetic imagers. If a scene or picture has been viewed for at least 30 or 40 seconds an eidetiker can "hold" his perception of it for several minutes afterward, and view the eidetic image as naturally and in as much detail as if the picture were still there (Jaensch,

1930; Haber and Haber, 1964). Some eidetic images seem indistinguishable from perceptions, even by objective criteria. Klüver (1928) found that 3 out of 20 eidetikers (that is less than 1% of the total population) reported bowing in an eidetic image of two parallel lines when the image was superimposed on a pattern of radiating lines. Haber gave his eidetic subjects a puzzle picture in which 2 schematic drawings of ocean scenes revealed a bearded man when superimposed; a few of his eidetic subjects were able to superimpose eidetic images of the 2 ocean scenes, and reported how the face sprung into view (Leask, Haber and Haber, 1968). Stromeyer and Psotka (1970) used Julesz patterns to test a young woman who possesses unusually vivid eidetic imagery. She was asked to recall via eidetic imagery a computer-generated pattern presented to her left eye several hours or days earlier while its matched pair was simultaneously presented to her right eye. The central three-dimensional square, reported by subjects who view the two patterns simultaneously, was clearly visible to this young woman.

In these situations, there is perfect fusion (or integration) of an image with a sensory perception, and the image functions almost like a sensory impression.

Thus it seems that every perceptual, and perhaps every sensory experience, can be duplicated by imagery in at least a few exceptional individuals. However, as one proceeds from the extreme eidetiker or mnemonist, through the less extreme eidetiker, the vivid imager, and finally the poor imager (cf. Sheehan, 1966b), it is increasingly difficult to reinstitute a facsimile of a perceptual experience through imagery alone. The extreme eidetiker or mnemonist may voluntarily produce constructions which mimic a perceptual experience, even showing sensory qualities. For most subjects, however, it is these sensory qualities which help to reveal a given experience as objective or perceptual.

DISTINCTIONS BETWEEN IMAGERY AND PERCEPTION

There seems to be a special sharpness in perception of edges and boundary changes, which give a perception special qualities of clarity and focus. This was noted by Sheehan (1966a) whose subjects reported an imaged yellow square to be dimmer, smaller, and more blurred than the original; and it was described by Brooks (1967), whose subjects used an imaged matrix to solve a task effectively, but remarked that they did not actually "see" the lines of the matrix.

A novel approach to the relationship of imagery and perception is observed in the investigations of Antrobus and Singer (Antrobus, Singer, and Greenberg, 1966; Antrobus, Coleman, and Singer, 1967; Antrobus, 1968). In their work they did not limit consideration to imagery, but included all types of mind-wandering (defined as "task-irrelevant thoughts"), while restricting the perceptual task to simple signal detection. They were not trying to demonstrate the similarity of the two processes, but rather to identify the reciprocity of these functions; with a demanding signal detection task, they measured less mind-wandering; if the signal detection task was easier, more daydreaming was observed. In these experiments, external and internal phenomena were quite different, although even here some subjects had difficulty deciding, for example, if the image of a waterfall was related to the signal tone or not. Antrobus (1968) tried to circumvent these issues by careful pre-training and instruction with his subjects, so they followed specific rules concerning ways to distinguish the task-related from the task-irrelevant thoughts.

Antrobus' research restricted perception to signal detections, just as the research previously reported focused on imagined replicas of sensory phenomena; use of such restricted operational definitions of imagery and perception reveals a clear dividing line between internal and external processes. Only in exceptional individuals or occasional instances is this dividing line breached. However, other research suggests that when a perceptual experience depends on complex central integrative events, and when the image depends more on perceptual than on sensory qualities, (e.g., Bartlett, 1932) far more similarities are found, and they tend to be more general over the population sampled.

CONDITIONED HALLUCINATIONS

For example, Scripture (1896) set up a threshold discrimination task. Using stimuli in all sensory modalities (a dim dot, a faint tone, a subtle odor, slight pressure, etc.), he asked each subject to indicate the moment he could detect the stimulus. Scripture also ran "catch" trials during which no stimulus was present; in these instances, subjects nevertheless reported "sensations," leading Scripture to assert that they "hallucinated" the stimulus.

Leuba (1940) conditioned 17 subjects under hypnosis by presenting, for example, a bell followed by a bright light. When the subject was wakened and a bell was sounded, the subject reported "seeing" a light. All but 1 of the 17 subjects reported such "conditioned hallucinations" in a variety of sense modes: auditory, tactile, visual, and olfactory.

Ellson (1941, 1942) studied this phenomenon without hypnosis; a light signaled the onset of a faint tone, and after many trials subjects began to report hearing the tone when only the light had been present. Ellson (1941) was able to demonstrate this effect reliably, although Kelley (1934) was unable to produce it with visual stimuli and a signaling tone.

KÜLPE AND PERKY

An original study, reported by Külpe in 1902, was partially replicated by Perky in 1910. In Külpe's work, each of 11 subjects was placed in a dark room facing a narrow wall. Onto this wall a lighted square, which could be varied as to size, brightness, and duration, was placed from time to time. Any statement made by the subject concerning any visual event was noted and scored as a "test," and the subject's attribution of the experience to an objective or subjective source was duly recorded. Each attribution was noted as a correct attribution of an objective event (a "hit")[2] or as an "error." Errors included false alarms, doubtful false alarms, doubtful attributions of stimulus events, and misses. While there were great individual differences, Külpe was especially impressed with the following observations: first, that subjects tended to have more false alarms, or showed a tendency to "objectivize," so doubtful events were usually classified as objective or external. He considered that this was in part due to the fact they they expected objective events, in part to the fact that it is biologically adaptive to recognize an external event. Second, many experiences included both "objective" and "subjective" components, for example; the square was seen to change color, to grow or shrink in size, to move about the room, or to take on new qualities and details, and entoptic phenomena appeared alone or combined with the projected square. However, subjects were never able to separate out the subjective from the objective portions; the experience was attributed *in toto* to an objective or subjective source. Third, the clues subjects used to differentiate objective from subjective events were variable, and frequently followed accepted philosophical assumptions, images being misty and vague, and percepts being clearer and more stable; but these were not reliable discriminanda. Fourth, subjects who were found (on other tests) to have more vivid imagery seemed to have more errors in these tests, and showed much less sensitivity (d') together with an extremely bold guessing strategy; the subject with the weakest imagery had the highest sensitivity and the most conservative criterion. Finally, when these experiments were replicated on 2 subjects,[3] whose hands were enclosed in a tunnel and touched on pressure spots with a variety of punctiform instruments, essentially similar results were obtained.

Perky's classic experiment (1910) was based on Külpe's study. Külpe had noted that the subjects tended to give more objective reports, and suggested that this might be because they expected objective stimuli; Perky wanted to determine if more subjective reports would be obtained when subjects expected only imagery. Her 29 subjects were asked to imagine common items while regarding a fixation point in the center of a window. Behind the window was an apparatus which permitted the projection of forms that mimicked the common images in shape and color, that had fuzzy edges, and oscillated slightly. The subject was told what to image, then the form was gradually brightened to about threshold brightness, and was removed as soon as he began to describe his image. Except when there were errors in the procedure, for example, when the assistant forgot to extinguish the

---

[2] Some of Külpe's descriptive language has been converted to standard signal detection terminology for greater clarity.

[3] One was Von Frey.

projection on cue, all observers confused the forms with their own images. These subjects, who did not expect stimuli to be shown, never reported that *any* "objective" signals were present; however, the images they described often resembled these undetected stimuli.

Külpe's subjects had demonstrated a clear tendency toward "objectivization"; many events that were wholly or partly dependent on subjective imagery and fantasy were mistakenly assumed to be objective. These false objectivizations occurred in 10% of the trials, and 2% more were doubtful. Külpe suggested that the main reason for this was a simple one: that subjects in fact expected to be shown objective phenomena. Nevertheless, there were some instances where objective events were mistakenly considered imaginary ("misses" of the signal). Külpe listed only 46 instances out of a grand total of 3464 visual trials, about 1.3%; in addition there were 202 instances (6%) where subjects expressed doubtful judgments and the origin was a visual stimulus. With the tactile stimuli, there were even fewer instances.

Perky's experiment was quite different. She tried to increase the occurrence of these false subjective attributions by building up an "imaginative consciousness." Using a technique derived in part from Külpe's, she instructed her observers so that they expected only subjective or imaginary experiences; and this method was so successful that although stimuli were present on every trial all subjects experienced and described all their percepts as imaginary. Thus, "misses" or "false subjectivizations," which occurred in Külpe's data about 1% of the time (or 7% including doubtful judgments), occurred 100% of the time in Perky's data. All the observers failed to recognize that an external stimulus was present. They formed an image which included both past experiences and some qualities of the stimulus, and yet judged that the constructed experience was entirely imaginary. With practised observers, some reported that the images were quite unusual, and were more like afterimages. Some decided unequivocally that no stimulus had been present; others seemed to have doubts which were never resolved. Thus one observer commented that "if I hadn't known I was imagining, should have thought it real (p. 433)," and another said, "it seems strange, because you see so many colors, and know that they are in your mind, and yet they look like shadows (p. 432)." Most, however, asserted that it "felt like" an image, they "could feel it formed in my mind—came right out of me (p. 433)."

This aspect of Perky's experiment, the decision that subjects make as to whether a stimulus is "real" or not, has been extensively investigated in our laboratory. Once it was established that Perky's findings could be replicated, a series of experiments was begun which investigated the parameters of the decision that subjects made; attributing a total sensory—cognitive experience either to an internal or to an external source. Between Külpe's report of less than 1% subjective attributions and Perky's report of 100% was a large area for exploration.

SEGAL EXPERIMENTS

Expectancy. It should be made clear, first, that this area is in fact quite limited. In the early replications, using the suspicious, pragmatic students who populated our campuses in the late 1950's and early 1960's, who had not been "turned on" and were embarrassed at the instruction to describe their inner experiences, it was rarely possible to replicate Perky's unanimously "subjective" results. Students initially described a construction that combined their imagery with the stimulus, and reported it as subjective; after 2 or 3 additional images, they frequently began to observe that a stimulus was present. A slight increase in the intensity of the stimulus would immediately reveal to the subject that a stimulus was present.

However, the subjects' attitudes could be manipulated experimentally. If a subject was given a placebo and told it was a "relaxant" that would make him less critical, and if he "reacted" to the placebo and accepted the suggested effect, he became less critical, and more likely to assert that only an image was present and not a stimulus. Even if the intensity of the stimulus was raised, he simply attributed this to the "drug" which was making his imagery more vivid, and failed to use it as a cue to alter his judgment. Conversely, if the subject resisted the suggestion of the placebo and failed to "react" to it, then he became more suspicious and critical and was more likely to detect the stimulus, even at lower intensity levels (Segal and Nathan, 1964) (see Table 1).

If the subject was asked to assume a supine position, a body position ordinarily associated with relaxation, imagery, dreams, and other internal events, he failed to notice most of the stimuli; if he was sitting, the stimuli were detected more often. And if he was standing, a posture associated with action and direct involvement with the physical world, the threshold was lowest of all, and the greatest number of stimuli were detected (Segal and Glicksman, 1967).

In these experiments, the results seemed largely attributable to the fact that subjects did not expect any stimuli. A direct test of this observation was necessary.

Twenty-four subjects were seated under the standard hood (Fig. 1), and while regarding the diffuse, vinyl surface ("like the unvarying background of the high-altitude pilot, deep-sea diver, or arctic explorer"), were informed that we were interested in the quality of their imagery. The subjects were asked to image 6 items successively; unknown to them, 4 of the images were accompanied by stimuli. After this, they were informed that some stimuli had been shown during some of the images, and they were asked to give a retrospective yes–no report, stating whether or not they thought stimuli had been shown for each of the 6 images. In the second part of the study, the subjects were asked for 6 more images; this time, however, they knew stimuli might be shown, and were asked after each image if a stimulus had been present. Again, 4 of the 6 images were accompanied by

TABLE 1

Experiment	Procedure	No. of subjects
Segal & Nathan (1964) Placebo study	Slides projected through window, 6 colored shapes for stimuli, 6 images. Placebo given. Inquiry at end	7 5 5
Segal (unpubl.) (1965) Thirst study	Ganzfeld-type hood. Stimuli were photographs of objects. Continu- ous reports on imagery, with occasional stimuli introduced. Inquiry at end. Same Ss tested thirsty and sated	8 7 8 7
Segal (1968a) Thirst study II	Ganzfeld-type hood. Stimuli were photographs, 20 images. Inquiry at end. Different Ss for thirsty and sated conditions	6 7 6 7
Segal & Glicksman (1967) Body position	Large Ganzfeld hood. Stimuli were photographs, 18 images. Inquiry at end. Same Ss tested in all positions	26 26 26
Segal & Gordon (1969) Effects of infor- mation	Exp. I: Ganzfeld hood. Colored figures for stimuli, 6 images. Same Ss for both conditions	24 24
	Exp. II: Cone-shaped hood with small screen. Stimuli were colored figures, 15 images. Same Ss for both conditions; but brighter stimuli for half, dim for half	24 24 12 12
Segal (1968b) Different methods of inquiry	Cone-shaped hood with screen; only two images requested Colored figure present with one; same Ss for both conditions	32 32
Segal & Fusella (1969) Mode of stimulus onset	Cone-shaped hood with screen. Different geometric figures, 40 images. Inquiry after each image	 16 16

Summary of Experimental Data, 1964–1970

Experimental conditions	Imagery tasks				Discrimination tasks			
	Hits	False alarms	d'	Lx	Hits	False alarms	d'	Lx
Control Ss	.21				.99+			
Placebo nonreactors	.33							
Placebo reactors	.19							
Thirsty: "Tolerant for ambiguity" Ss	.78				.99+			
"Intolerant for ambiguity" Ss	.13							
Sated: "Tolerant for ambiguity" Ss	.58							
"Intolerant" S	.28							
Thirsty: "Tolerant for ambiguity" Ss	.19	.13	.25	1.28	.99+			
"Intolerant" Ss	.03	.05	−.24	.66				
Sated: "Tolerant" Ss	.13	.09	.21	1.30				
"Intolerant" Ss	.36	.02	1.70	7.73				
Supine	.29				.95+			
Sitting	.49							
Standing	.64							
Perky replication: inquiry at end	.38	.15	.74	1.61	.93			
"Informed"; inquiry after each image	.66	.04	2.03	14.30				
Experimenter projected slides	.55	.05	1.77	11.25	.85	.050	2.68	18.78
Subject projected slides	.62	.05	1.94	12.57				
Brighter stimuli	.86	.06	2.63	14.59	.94	.044	3.26	1.28
Dimmer stimuli	.57	.04	1.93	16.20	.75	.034	2.50	4.21
Inquiry at end, uninformed	.03				.98			
Informed, forced choice judgment	.63							
Exp. I:								
Gradual onset of stimuli	.40	.081	1.14	2.56	.81	.047	2.56	2.72
Immediate onset, 3 sec	.48	.080	1.61	3.87	.88	.044	2.87	2.15

TABLE 1 (Continued)

Experiment	Procedure	No. of subjects
		16
		16
Segal & Fusella (1970a) Audiovisual effects	Cone-shaped hood with screen	
	Exp. I: 6 sessions, each with 48 auditory, 48 visual images. Visual signal, auditory signal, no signal presented 32 times each	8
		8
	Exp. II: 8 sessions, each with 63 auditory, 63 visual images. Visual signal, auditory signal, no signal presented 42 times each	6
		6
Segal & Fusella (1971) Six sense modes	Three sessions, each with 64 visual images, 32 auditory, 8 gustatory, 8 olfactory, 8 kinesthetic, 8 tactile. Background "noise," with figured stimulus on ½ the trials	20

stimuli. Finally, all the 8 stimuli were shown in a simple threshold procedure, and it was established that most of them were clearly visible. Subjects were far more likely to be correct in the second condition, where they expected a stimulus and had already seen some stimuli, than in the first condition, where they expected only images (Segal and Gordon, 1969).

Signal Detection Measures of Imagery. To measure their relative accuracy more efficiently, signal detection methods were adopted (see Swets, 1964; Green and Swets, 1966). It is possible, statistically, to separate out a subject's bias or guessing strategy from his basic sensory sensitivity. His sensitivity or d' refers to the difference (in standard deviation units) between two hypothetical functions; one representing the curve for reception of background noise (no stimulus), and one representing the curve for reception of the signal. In this experiment, d' was .74 in the uninformed imaging condition, 2.03 in the informed condition. This difference

TABLE 1 (Continued)

Experimental conditions	Imagery tasks				Discrimination tasks			
	Hits	False alarms	d'	Lx	Hits	False alarms	d'	Lx
Exp. II:								
Gradual onset	.49	.038	1.75	4.83	.65	.024	2.36	6.54
Immediate 2 sec	.45	.054	1.48	3.61	.74	.067	2.14	2.53
Visual signal: blue arrow								
Visual imagery	.60	.109	1.48	2.06	.73	.094	1.93	1.97
Auditory imagery	.62	.084	1.68	2.47	.64	.087	1.72	2.36
Auditory signal: harmonica								
Visual imagery	.87	.006	3.64	12.44	.93	.009	3.84	5.52
Auditory imagery	.82	.013	3.14	7.38	.90	.002	4.16	27.68
Visual signal: green bars								
Visual imagery	.61	.078	1.70	2.63	.82	.042	2.64	2.93
Auditory imagery	.63	.036	2.13	4.78	.80	.023	2.84	5.00
Auditory signal: 250 cps tone								
Visual imagery	.67	.037	2.23	4.48	.83	.032	2.81	3.53
Auditory imagery	.61	.067	1.78	2.96	.79	.034	2.63	3.82
Visual imagery	.76	.105	1.99	1.67				
Auditory imagery	.79	.078	2.23	1.98	.82	.040	2.67	3.05
All other modes	.78	.088	2.13	1.85	.82	.043	2.63	2.87

was very large and significant. However, equally impressive was the fact that in the final threshold discrimination task where there was no imagery, the subjects' d' or sensitivity for the stimulus was estimated to be more than 3 SD units, significantly greater than the 2.03 obtained in the informed condition (see Table 1).

This led to the surprising conclusion that while relaxation and instructions had a marked effect, apparently a mental image by itself could somehow raise the threshold or block perception of a stimulus, even when the subject was familiar with the stimulus and knew that a stimulus might be shown.

This seemed sufficiently important that in subsequent studies any possible artifacts which might influence this result were controlled for, in attempting to evaluate the pure effect of an image on detection of a signal.

The large plastic hood used in previous work, which provided a virtual Ganzfeld around the subject's head as well as a screen on which the stimuli could be

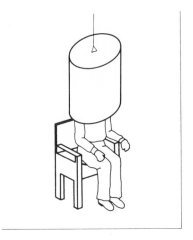

Fig. 1. Hood used in imagery experiments.

back-projected, was replaced by a plastic cylinder with a small screen at one end
(Fig. 2). This controlled for the Ganzfeld effect, which makes it difficult to locate a
stimulus, even without imagery, under otherwise ideal detection conditions in a
limitless field (Miller, 1960).

As the screen subtended a visual angle of about 16°, it provided a simple,
defined background which the subject could scan readily. A single stimulus was
presented for 2 seconds on each trial; usually the stimulus was a simple, colored
geometric form. Fifty to one hundred preliminary trials familiarized a subject with
this stimulus and permitted the experimenter to adjust the stimulus intensity to a
level where it could be detected about 65–85% of the time. Then a standard
discrimination procedure was held with several hundred trials—half with the
stimulus present, half with the stimulus absent. Next, the subject was asked to
imagine something, and as soon as he signaled that he "had" an image, the projector
was turned on.[4] Again, half the time the stimulus was present, half the time no
stimulus was shown. There were several hundred trials with imagery, and then a
second discrimination procedure to ensure that subjects' sensitivity had not
changed during the testing.

This general procedure was established over a series of experiments and with
it we have reliably and repeatedly demonstrated that sensory sensitivity (d') is

_____

[4]In the studies reported here, the stimulus was sometimes presented just before,
sometimes just after, the subject reported experiencing the image. The precise temporal
relationship of stimulus onset to the development and fading of the image is an experimental
question; research on this issue is now being planned.

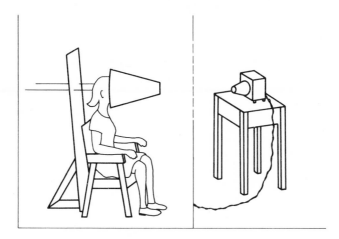

Fig. 2. Hood used in later imagery experiments. The projector was usually located in a separate room, on the other side of a window.

poorer when a subject is imaging than when he is not. This effect was obtained when subjects expected the stimulus, when they projected it themselves, and even when they merely "imaged" the item and were not asked to describe it verbally. (Segal and Gordon, 1969; Segal and Fusella, 1969). It was found that whether onset of the stimulus was gradual, so that it brightened and then faded over a total of 6 seconds, or whether the stimulus was projected at maximum intensity for a briefer period, the image still interfered with signal detection; and so long as brightness over time was constant, the mode of stimulus onset did not alter the phenomenon (Segal and Fusella, 1969). If a simple grid was present on every trial, constituting the "noise," and the stimulus appeared in the center of this grid on the "signal" trials, even though subjects presumably were alerted by the grid, their sensitivity for distinguishing the signal from the grid continued to be poorer when an image was also present (Segal and Fusella, 1971).

Finally, subjects were asked for both auditory and visual images, and their task involved detecting both auditory and visual signals. It was reliably demonstrated that auditory images interfered more with detection of auditory signals, and visual images with detection of visual signals. This was especially important, for it demonstrated that imagery did not have a diffuse effect, distracting the observer's attention. Rather, imagery had a very precise effect, which depended on the modality in which it was experienced. (Segal and Fusella, 1970a). Following this, it was shown that visual imagery interfered specifically with a visual signal, and that auditory, gustatory, olfactory, tactile, and kinesthetic imagery all have similar and much slighter influence on d' for a visual signal (Segal and Fusella, 1971).

ASSIMILATION VS. ACCOMMODATION

Most of these findings can readily be explained in terms of the distinction between assimilation and accommodation. The term "assimilation" was borrowed from Piaget, as he had borrowed it from biology (1951). He noted how new experiences may, in certain situations, be assimilated to a current need or interest. An example is that of a child who watches a cat walking along a fence; the child takes a small box, moves it along a table edge, and states, "this is the cat on the fence." This is not simply a metaphor: the child ignores the characteristics of the box, that it is square, small, made of cardboard, etc., noting only that in being moved along a table, its progress resembles that of the cat. The child ignores all special qualities of the box except the ones that can be assimilated to his current cognition; thus the process of assimilation helps him to understand the movement of the cat. To apprehend the qualities of the box *qua* box, a different approach would be taken, and he would *accommodate* his actions to them.

In similar fashion, a perceptual event may involve the assimilation of sensory input to an intended image or idea. In this process, the unique qualities of the sensory input are lost, because the input is processed only insofar as it relates to the dominant image. If a given observer is trying to apprehend the salient characteristics of a given stimulus, then his behavior is accommodative, and ideas or inner constructions are suggested by the properties of the stimulus. But if the observer is attending to his inner images or experiences, then the sensory input may be assimilated to a concurrent image; in such instances, only the relevant features of the physical stimulus will be processed, and even these may be markedly transformed.

The task of signal detection is basically an accommodative task. The more clearly a subject appreciates the unique qualities of the stimulus and the precise task requirements, the more accurate he will be. Imagery is an assimilational task; to construct a good image, the observer must recruit any past memories as well as random sensory input to the construction of the image. If the condition, for example, relaxation, a supine body posture, a signal in the same sensory mode as the image, tends to favor the assimilative tendencies, then the sensory input is assimilated to the image, and is less available as a cue for signal detection. On the other hand, if the observer is induced to react accommodatively to a signal by his alert body posture, or because the cues from the stimulus appear in a different sense mode from his image, then he is more likely to process the signal as an event separate from his image, and sensory sensitivity is increased.

ASSIMILATION

However, the concept of assimilation has certain implications, which must be made explicit and evaluated. Central to this concept is the assumption that sensory input can be fused with an image, even that the image may be constructed around an undetected physical signal. If an image by definition occurs in the absence of a physical stimulus, then it hardly makes sense to state that the image is based on a physical stimulus. If the image is defined as occurring in the absence of an *appropriate* or *relevant* stimulus, the inconsistency is largely evaded.

The next portion of the paper will, therefore, question the former definition. Empirical data will show that hallucinations and images cannot be characterized by the absence of a stimulus, but rather that in many, perhaps all, instances they depend on sensory input. Sometimes the sensory information is endogenous, sometimes exogenous in origin. Always it is assimilated to and transformed by the observer's own past experiences, expectancies, and drives.

HALLUCINATIONS BASED ON AN ENDOGENOUS INPUT

There are many recorded instances of hallucinations or images that seem to occur in the absence of stimulation. Careful review of much of the data, however, suggests that there always is sensory input, sometimes endogenous in origin, but transmitted along the sensory channels, and the resulting image is simply a construction, with a central core of sensory input elaborated by the expectancies and past experiences.

Klüver (1966), in his classic report on mescal hallucinations, commented on the "hallucinatory constants," the reporting of hallucinations which related to certain specific forms, for example, (a) grating or honeycomb, (b) cobweb, (c) tunnel, or (d) spiral. These constants have also been observed in schizophrenic hallucinations and alcoholic delirium, during drug-induced hallucinations, and hallucinations accompanying certain neurological diseases (Horowitz, 1967). Horowitz found that a sample of normal adults reported many of the same form constants after pressing on the eyeballs, suffering a blow on the head, during periods of fever, isolation, alcoholic intoxication, extreme fatigue, and also as part of hypnagogic imagery. They typically report figures of stars, wheels, specks, snakes, and fire (Horowitz, 1964). Klüver, Horowitz, and others suggested that these are cognitive elaborations of simple, universal entoptic phenomena.

Auditory hallucinations are far more common in schizophrenic and alcoholic hallucinations; and they may have a comparable basis. Saravay and Pardes (1967) suggested that there are local effects in the middle ear, which underlie these phenomena. During states of altered consciousness, during alcoholic intoxication as well as withdrawal, drug-induced reactions, schizophrenic hallucinations, even during sleep and states of fatigue, slight shifts in the states of contraction of the muscles of the middle ear may yield sound sources which ordinarily, like the entoptic phenomena, pass unnoticed; however, in states of lowered, and perhaps also in states of heightened arousal (see West, 1962, Chapter 26, pp. 275-291), these sounds do register in the brain. Generally, these entotic sounds, like the entoptic phenomena, are modified by central expectancies, past memories, or current cognitions, resulting in complex and meaningful hallucinations.

SENSORY DEPRIVATION

Many of these effects could be studied empirically, when it was found that similar phenomena were spontaneously reported by subjects who were subjected to conditions of perceptual restriction or "sensory deprivation."

In the earlier experiments of this type (e.g., Bexton, Heron, and Scott, 1954), an aim was to reduce information bearing sensory input by filling the auditory channels with white noise, and flooding the visual channels with diffuse, unpatterned light. Other later investigators (e.g., Shurley, 1962, Chapter 14, pp. 153–154) tried to reduce the absolute level of stimulation by using blackout goggles, stuffing the ears, even suspending the subject in water. While some sensory input inevitably was present in both procedures, the amount of patterned or representational stimulation was effectively attenuated with either method. The early reports suggested, and later studies confirmed, that individuals sometimes experienced hallucinations and vivid imagery in the virtual absence of stimulation.

The first paper on sensory restriction by Bexton, Heron, and Scott (1954) reported on 22 male college students, who lay on comfortable beds for up to 48 hours. Translucent goggles transmitted diffuse light; auditory and tactile stimulation was restricted. The first 8 subjects spontaneously reported curious perceptual experiences, which one described as "having a dream while awake." The last 14 subjects were systematically questioned, and all reported some visual effects: the visual field changed from dark to light, or there were dots, lines, and simple geometrical patterns; occasional subjects reported "wallpaper patterns" and isolated figures, even complex integrated scenes. Bexton *et al.* commented on the similarity of the complex experiences to mescal and migraine hallucinations, as well as to hallucinations in aged patients and during febrile illnesses.

These reports of "hallucinations" occurring in the apparent absence of sensory input excited considerable interest, and led to many replications. Was the brain somehow constructing these impressions to provide autostimulation in the absence of sensory stimulation? Did they depend on certain specific aspects of the deprivation experience? Some 16 years later, it may be possible to answer some of these questions.

There were many reports of hallucinations which clearly developed around some minimal sensory input. Imagery was experienced by all of 11 subjects who were placed in a water-filled tank with maximum attenuation of sensory input. Shurley noted that "under conditions of very low levels of sensory input, one can hear extremely faint sounds to which one ordinarily does not attend. For example, the faint sound of water trickling or distant plumbing became the nidus for one man's auditory experience of shore birds crying; this was accompanied by the picture of a seashore he once knew, and the experience was so vivid that he thought he smelled the salt air (Shurley, 1962, p.156)." Faint light patterns were seen by 2 subjects, described as an X-ray by a medical student, as a Rorschach card by a psychologist; but both subjects were convinced that their perceptual experience was real and presented by the experimenter (Silverman, Cohen, Bressler, and Shmavonian, 1962, Chapter 11, pp. 125–134).

In many instances, the simple forms, flashes of colors and lights, dots, swirls, or lines, can be attributed directly either to entoptic effects or to afterimages which can occur if the subject blinks his eyes when he is exposed to diffuse light. In many instances, the more complex forms may be derivatives of these and other endogenous effects, elaborated by central memories and expectancies.

It is not always feasible to compare the many publications on sensory isolation, since each experimenter used a different method to elicit descriptions of inner experiences and different classification systems and statistics to report these data. Furthermore, variations among subjects and in theoretical predilection of the experimenters often profoundly influence the nature of the data. Zuckerman (1969, Chapter 4, pp. 85–125) in trying to summarize the research data on hallucinations during sensory deprivation, has tried to draw inferences from this research, and it is difficult to improve on his analysis.

After reviewing all of the literature on hallucinations, Zuckerman concluded that *all* simple invariant sensory fields produce "reported visual sensations." Blackout goggles, which may make it difficult to project an image in front of one, may slightly restrict the frequency of visual reports; however, the watertank technique, which reduces all physical stimulation as much as possible and which also uses blackout goggles, seems to induce at least as many reports of visual phenomena as any other method. With these possible exceptions, it seems to make no difference whether the room is dark or lighted, or whether the subject is wearing halved ping-pong balls or other goggles admitting diffuse light; approximately the same frequencies of visual effects are reported. Only if the subject is exposed to intermittent or fluctuating stimulation is the frequency of these reports significantly reduced.

While these visual reports, especially the complex sensations, seem to resemble dream fragments or hypnagogic imagery, it has not been possible to establish that they occur more frequently during states of drowsiness or sleep. On the contrary, there is some evidence that visual sensations are more often *reported* during states of high or medium arousal (Zuckerman, 1969), although at least one researcher believes that the *phenomena themselves* are more likely to occur during hypnagogic or drowsy states (see Ziskind, 1965). The critical experiment on this issue is not available, as it still defies experimental ingenuity to obtain full reports from a drowsy subject.

Many interpretations of these data are possible. A few obvious but important conclusions can be drawn. First, neither homogeneity nor a low level of external stimulation results in the absence of sensation. Second, in the absence of patterned external stimulation, reported experiences range all the way from blank fields to complex visions and scenes in which the observer feels he plays an active part and which are accepted as veridical. Third, while these experiences do not usually resemble psychotic hallucinations, they are very similar to afterimages, illusions, hypnagogic imagery, dreams, and even drug-induced hallucinations (Zuckerman, 1969).

These phenomena may have appeared during sensory deprivation because minor variations in the physical world as well as minor intraorganismic variations assume such importance in a restricted sensory environment. Sometimes, these endogenous effects are coded in relatively pure form, and appear simply as clicks or whirring sounds, as dots, splashes, or networks of colored light; sometimes, especially after a more prolonged period of sensory deprivation, subjects report a more complex sensory–cognitive experience. These events may begin with virtually the same endogenous sensory input, but because of the special state of the brain, this input is elaborated into a detailed, perceptual-like event, which is often classified as a hallucination by the experimenter.

SUBLIMINAL PERCEPTION

A completely different methodological technique has been found useful in the direct study of perceptual events of this type. An alert and responsive normal human subject is presented with a very minor variation in the physical world, a variation that, like the entoptic and entotic phenomena, is usually subliminal, and then the subject is asked to report on his dreams or images. Extensive research on such "subliminal perception" reveals that a minimal stimulus, presented outside the area of focal awareness, frequently influences a subsequent image or fantasy. The stimulus is considered outside awareness when it is presented too briefly to be fully apprehended, too dimly to be clearly perceived, or peripheral to the central attention of the subject so that the subject fails to report that he perceives it.

In the original exploration, Pötzl (1917, tr. 1960) asked subjects to describe a complex picture, and then to note down any dreams that occurred during the subsequent night's sleep. He found that elements and details in the picture which they had *failed* to report emerged in the dreams. This experiment was repeated (Fisher, 1954; Fisher and Paul, 1959; Shevrin and Luborsky, 1958) with equivocal findings; the number of unreported items in the subsequent images and dreams did *not* exceed the number of reported items, although it seemed impressive that any unreported items emerged.

This technique was subsequently modified: the stimulus was made so dim and ambiguous or reduced to a tachistoscopic presentation so brief that *no* elements could be reported. Instead of reporting dreams the next day, subjects reported on their imagery immediately after the stimulus was presented. Like the unreported details and endogenous effects, these degraded stimuli seemed to figure in the subjects' descriptions of their imagery. In these studies, control conditions using a brief flash of light were introduced and judges tried to select which images followed the stimulus, which followed the control flash (Fisher and Paul, 1959; Fiss, Goldberg, and Klein, 1963; Klein, Spence, Holt, and Gourevitch, 1958). They were usually correct slightly, but significantly, above chance level.

There has been considerable controversy over the explanation of findings such as these. The results are usually significant, but not striking, and several writers have tried to discredit this entire line of research (Eriksen, 1960; Goldiamond, 1958; Neisser, 1967). I am suggesting that even when the stimulus was too brief for a subject to consciously experience it, even where he was unable to make a present–absent distinction, there was still some minimal responding in some of the retinal cells; this minimal input was sometimes taken up by and encoded as part of the ensuing cognitive experience.

That is, there is no such thing as an absolute threshold (cf. Swets, 1961); therefore a stimulus cannot be subthreshold or subliminal. Presumably, the stimuli used in the subliminal experiments had some minimal detectability which did not lead to a reliable detection report, but could be assimilated to ongoing cognitive processes.

ASSIMILATION IN KÜLPE'S AND PERKY'S RESEARCH

Some of the same phenomena may have been responsible for Külpe's finding. He noted that subjects sometimes reported a complex experience in which the projected square appeared to change colors, or to move about the room, and in some instances seemed so variable that subjects could no longer report whether it was an "objective" or a "subjective" experience. Külpe suggested that first the subjective and objective portions were fused into a single experience, then the entire experience was classified as either subjective or objective, but the parts could no longer be processed or classified separately. In these findings, it appears that a stimulus could create so slight a change in the pattern of sensory input that it was not processed as an objective signal, but such a stimulus might still be assimilated to a subjective cognitive production.

The same explanation can be applied to Perky's findings. In her data, also, the stimulus typically was not detected as such, and failed to emerge into conscious awareness, yet it also appeared transformed in the observer's concomitant imagery. Perky described in some detail how the images seemed to resemble the stimuli or, in some cases, to incorporate fragments of the stimulus:

One graduate observer apologized for her "poor imagination," and said she could get forms but not colors; as a matter of fact, she failed to see the color of the stimulus. Another graduate observer, who had had long experience in the laboratory and had worked to some extent with imagery, showed, both by the time of appearance of the image and by its characteristics (shape, position, size), that he was incorporating the perception in it, while he nevertheless supplied a context of pure imagery: the tomato was seen painted on a can; the book was a particular book whose title could be read; the lemon was lying on a table; the leaf was a pressed leaf with red markings on it. All the observers noted that the banana was on end and not as they had been supposing they thought of it. Some saw an elm leaf when they had been trying for a maple leaf (Perky, 1910, p. 432).

ASSIMILATION EFFECTS: SEGAL EXPERIMENTS

In the initial replication of Perky's study published in 1964 (Segal and Nathan), there was some evidence for assimilation. All of the 17 subjects were asked to imagine 6 simple items successively. The procedure here was similar to Perky's. On each trial, the subject was instructed to image a specific item while regarding a spot in a window, and as he began to describe his image, a facsimile of the item was projected at the spot. On those trials where the subject detected the projected stimulus, the accompanying image was *not* analyzed for assimilation; by definition, assimilation occurred only when the subject incorporated aspects of the stimulus into his image *without detecting* a change in the physical world. On review by the experimenter of the subjects' descriptions, 34 out of 52 images (or 65%) showed evidence of assimilation, with perhaps 6–8 more images showing equivocal signs. For example, an open book in a neutral or white color was the stimulus, and 5 out of 9 subjects described an open book with white pages, 1 described "two rectangles," and a seventh commented on the yellow pages. The eighth subject described a medieval hand-lettered book, and the ninth imaged a red book with green edges. Seven of these were scored as assimilations. Five out of 7 subjects described their banana as long and yellow and these were counted assimilations; the other two added brown spots. Several other subjects noted that the banana was horizontal when their imaged banana had been vertically positioned, and this was a clue which persuaded them that slides had been shown.

All this was interesting, but as far as experimental methodology was concerned, it was no advance over Titchener's laboratory. To begin with, there were no controls; if subjects are asked to imagine bananas, most will imagine long yellow objects. In the next few studies, attempts were made to develop adequate controls and more objective methods.

In the next study (Segal, 1965, unpubl., Table 2) subjects were seated under a large hood constructed of translucent vinyl (cf. Fig. 1). They were instructed to image different items while regarding the vinyl surface with their eyes open. A few seconds after directions to image were given, a dim slide was back-projected onto the vinyl surface. Two kinds of stimuli were used: some were congruent to the

TABLE 2
Judgments on Assimilation

Experiment	No. of subjects	No. of images/ subject	Character of stimuli	Frequency of correct stimulus detections	No. of judges	Informed or blind	% Correct judgments
Segal & Nathan, 1964	17	6	All images accompanied by congruent stimuli	.25	1	Informed	65[a]
Segal (unpubl.), 1965	15	10	Half with congruent stimuli, half with incongruent	.46	2	Informed	53[a]
Segal, 1968a	46	40	Half congruent; half incongruent	.18	3	Blind	49.7
Segal & Gordon, 1969	12	18	Half by geometric shape; half by nothing	.57	3	Blind	57
Segal & Fusella, 1969	32	40	Half by one stimulus; half by another	.44	3	Blind	55
	32	40	Half by one stimulus; one by nothing	.47	2	Blind	58
Segal, 1968b	32	2	One by stimulus; one by nothing	.13	2	Blind	41
Segal (unpubl.)	12	3	One by stimulus; two by nothing	.00	18	Blind	56
	12	3	One by stimulus; two by nothing	.00	18	Blind	57

[a]These are not strictly "correct," but refer to judges' decision that assimilation had occurred.

image, e.g., a butterfly was shown when the subject was asked to image a butterfly, and some were incongruent, e.g., an elephant was shown when the subject imaged a glass of iced tea. Two judges evaluated the images described, and judged that about half the images showed assimilation; they agreed on 63% of the judgments. Fully two-thirds of the incongruent combinations were considered by both judges to show some evidence of assimilation. For example, asked to image a city skyline, but shown a tomato, several subjects described the skyline with a round sun behind it, setting in a red sky.

In the next 4 studies, all subjects described the same images, but the experimental design provided that different subjects had different stimuli accompanying the same image. For example, all subjects might be told to image an elephant, but half would be shown the slide of an elephant and the other half would be shown a pair of eyeglasses; and so on. All descriptions of the images were tape-recorded, transcribed, and then grouped, so that all images of the elephant were placed together. Then judges were asked to sort through the images of the elephant, and try to guess which ones were accompanied by the elephant, and which by the eyeglasses. This was the first occasion where the judging was objective, and the judges made their decisions "blind." The results are shown in Table 2, and most are not especially impressive.

In the first study, the mean percentage of correct judgments was .497 for the 3 judges, almost precisely what would be predicted by chance. On a *post hoc* basis, however, there seemed somewhat more evidence for assimilation, findings which the judges had failed to use. Descriptions of the images were more likely to be the most typical or conventional view of the item when the congruent stimulus was presented; but during incongruent stimulations, the images tended to have idiosyncratic features, and the general form and color of the incongruent stimulus often appeared as background or as details. For example, shown a glass of iced tea, subjects imaged iced tea as either red or reddish brown, or else as transparent; shown an elephant, they tended to report on things in the iced tea: lemon, sugar, a spoon, mint, or a teabag. Asked to imagine a coke glass, it was more often described as the usual coke glass or with "Coca-Cola" written on it when subjects were shown a coke glass; when they were shown a white cup and saucer with coffee in it, they were more likely to describe the coke in a paper container.

In the subsequent experiment, a different hood was used with a smaller screen so the stimuli would be more likely to fall on or near the fovea; each image was accompanied by a simplified colored geometric form or by nothing. This time, the 3 judges, judging blind, all scored above chance, with 51, 58, and 63% correct. Again, a glance at the specific examples is interesting. Asked to imagine a pack of cigarettes, subjects shown a green square reported Salem or True brand cigarettes a quarter of the time, both of which are menthol brands which appear in a green package; subjects shown nothing never reported these brands. When a red circle was shown, subjects described a clock as orange or brass, and generally as a kitchen clock or alarm clock; whereas with no stimulus, subjects tended to describe grandfather clocks, cuckoo clocks, or other special antique clocks.

The next 2 experiments were very similar. In both, the hood with the small screen was used (see Fig. 2). Each subject was asked for the same 40 images, and the stimuli were colored geometric figures. Three judges, scoring blind, were correct 53, 54, and 57% of the time in one study; and 2 judges, scoring blind, were correct

56 and 59% of the time in the replication. In both studies, there seemed more evidence of assimilation when stimuli were introduced at a very low intensity and increased in brightness, than when stimuli were presented at a stable intensity level (Segal and Fusella, 1969a).

A pattern of 9 dots, 4 larger and 5 smaller, placed randomly in a circular display, was one of the stimuli used. When colored brown and presented while subjects were imaging a street, many described potholes in the street, dirty papers, and candy bar wrappers. When this same stimulus was presented, colored red, to subjects imaging a bicycle, several commented that it seemed like an old or battered bike, with rusty spots. The image of a doll was often described as being rigid when 2 red squares were shown; but with the stimulus of a green spiral, one subject reported a tiny doll with "twisty" arms and legs, and another described a cartoon-type doll, with long curls.

In the next 2 experiments, each subject reported on and described only 2 images. Judges compared the 2 images reported by each subject and tried to decide which one was accompanied by the stimulus. On the first experiment, the 2 judges scored below chance, 47 and 35% correct. In the succeeding experiment, subjects described and drew pictures of their images. Two different pairs of images were used, each accompanied by a different stimulus. For this judgment, ratings were obtained from 18 persons, who showed considerable variability in their scores, but averaged 56% correct with one stimulus, 57% with the other.

None of the experiments reported yields unequivocal evidence by itself, nevertheless, taken together, they begin to show a consistent pattern, and apparently, the phenomenon of assimilation does occur. There are certain rules one can extract from these data. Assimilation is more likely to be obtained when the stimulus is less intense, or when it is brightened gradually. It occurs less often when there is abrupt onset of the stimulus or when there is a brighter stimulus. Also, it seems that the general form and color of a stimulus are most likely to be assimilated to the image, and that the content of the stimulus rarely emerges. The basic image, especially its color, shading, details, or background, is often influenced by the stimulus. Sometimes the stimulus has a more profound (even physiognomic) effect which determines the qualitative features of the image—whether it is fresh and new, or dirty and rusted; whether a doll is rigid when squares are shown, or cartoon-like when the stimulus is a spiral. There is a clear tendency for the resulting image to be realistically probable. One unique subject fused an elephant to an image of iced tea, and reported imaging a caterpillar drinking iced tea. This type of image is probably more common with a schizophrenic population (Silverman, 1966); and among our normal sample, there were no other instances of such original or confabulated images.

Evidence has been garnered that is largely anecdotal, but at least consistent, suggesting that assimilation does occur. It is not clear at present whether assimilation is a relatively infrequent occurrence, which causes it to be infrequently found, or whether, although it is a fairly common occurrence, either the experimental conditions used or the method of measuring assimilation are fairly inefficient, which is why it has been possible to demonstrate it only infrequently.

THE REALITY DECISION

It may be that assimilation and accommodation are reciprocally related, and it seems possible that the reason subjects failed to detect the stimulus in the Perky-type situation is that the stimulus was assimilated to the image, and was therefore unavailable for detection. This explanation may be clearer if we consider another experiment which analyzed the decision process itself (Segal, 1968b).

Thirty-two subjects were asked to imagine two items: a violin and a plant. Unknown to them, during one of the images, the experimenter presented a slide of a red outline figure, resembling 2 squares with open bases. Afterward, subjects were asked if they thought anything had been projected during their imagery. All but one said no. Then they were told: "Something was placed on the screen during one of these images. Please guess where it occurred, during the image of the plant or of the violin." Twenty of the 32 subjects were able to guess correctly. However, when these subjects were asked *what* was shown, most guessed incorrectly that it was the item they imagined, i.e., the plant or the violin; when the stimulus was described to them (as "2 incomplete red squares") and they were asked to guess again, only 5 changed their guesses, but all changed from a correct to an incorrect guess. Subjects who made a correct choice on the first forced-choice procedure would report: "Before the image of a plant that I reported, I imagined a pot of geraniums—I think that was projected," or "The image I had of a plant was funny, so I think it was projected." When they were asked to describe what was shown, however, the subjects were confused. They would either report that they didn't know, or else would say, with some surprise, "Well, it was the plant," or "It was the violin." When the stimulus was described to them, the description did not match what they had seen, for the physical stimulus was simply not processed as two incomplete red squares; it was processed as the bow and body of the reddish brown fiddle, or a plant in a dark red pot with designs on it. At this point, the subjects could not recover the physical stimulus, since they never, in fact, saw it. The sensory input registered, but it was coded as part of the image; the subject can review his subjective experience, but he cannot restore the original sensory input and later code or process it in a different way.

These findings were bolstered by a replication of the experiment. The procedure was similar, but 64 subjects reported on 3 images, a parrot, a tree, and an abstract painting, and had to draw each image as well as describe it. None of them were aware that anything had been projected (those who did report projections were excluded from the analysis), and they were able to guess only at a chance level. Half the subjects were then shown the stimulus again, and several changed to a correct guess, so accuracy climbed from 28% to 41%; for the other half, the stimulus was described in geometric terms as "a triangular-shaped design of 3 green bars," and many subjects changed from a correct to an incorrect guess, so accuracy for these 32 subjects fell from 38% to 16% (Segal and Fusella, 1970b). When the same stimulus was reprojected, it could be coded as part of a parrot or a tree, and compared with the image of the tree or of the parrot. However, when subjects had to compare the experimenter's verbal coding of the input as "3 green bars" to their own image, they could not realize that the two different codings were based on the same sensory input.

For the sensory input does not depict an external stimulus; it merely gives clues out of which the observer constructs a personal experience. Sensory input is always present, and whether a conscious subjective image approximates an external stimulus and so is called a "perception" or fails to match any consensually valid external stimulus and so is called an "image" or "hallucination," the process involved in both experiences is similar. Both the "perceptual" experience and the "imagery" experience are in fact constructions.

How does one distinguish an image from a perception? If image and percept are so similar, how can we be so efficient in discriminating between them?

In most situations, this distinction does not present a problem; most of the time, we seem to make this distinction correctly and almost automatically. Because the decision is made correctly such a high proportion of the time, it is sometimes assumed that the decision is somehow immanent or "given" (e.g., Bruner, 1957; Attneave, 1962, pp. 619–659), as if a given experience carries a special label revealing it to have been transmitted by the sense receptors. It seems more reasonable to assume that the decision is usually correct only because so many factors, such as the qualities of the sensory input, certain quantitative and qualitative characteristics of the emergent experience, the confluence of input from different sense modalities, and contextual probabilities inferred from many past experiences, enter into it.

The idea that qualities of the sensory input unequivocally indicate the presence of a "real" external object must be wrong. Sensory input is constantly being fed into the central nervous system. It seems that under the influence of certain drugs, such as alcohol, the retinal cells may fire; they also appear to fire with greater frequency when the eyes are *not* stimulated by a physical signal than when they are (Granit, 1955). If peripheral sensory cells can fire when the initiating cause is an event in the external physical world, when it is an internal change, and when nothing has occurred, then there is no advantage for the organism to be able to ascertain at what level in the sensory tract the firing commenced. Therefore, presumably, such a distinction is not made.

A further reason for this may be considered. A perception may in certain instances occur when an intelligent and experienced observer is able to "make sense" out of very minimal physical stimulation, as when an Australian aborigine infers (or constructs) an approaching convoy from the sensory stimulation provided by a few flecks of dust in the distance. In some instances an image may occur when random sensory events are incorporated into a pattern, as when the traveler on the desert mistakes a particular pattern caused by light shining on a flat stretch of sand for a water hole and even sees trees around it. It may be that more sensory input initiated by external changes is present in the cognitive experience which we label as a "mirage" than in the aborigine's perception; in these examples, the amount of exogenous sensory input may not yield accurate information as to the reality or nonreality of an event. Therefore, one must assume that it is adaptively beneficial if the reality decision depends on other sources of information.

A given organism experiences a sensory-cognitive event at a specific point in time and in a specific state of consciousness. The identical event experienced during guerilla fighting in the Vietnam rice paddies, while lying in one's bed at home sound asleep, while sitting in a fitted chair in an experimental psychological laboratory, or while walking to work in the morning becomes 4 separate events, each with its own set of probabilities and assumptions about reality.

Thus the decision concerning reality is essentially a probability decision. The central "operator," to borrow a common term from information theory, makes an initial guess as to the reality of a given experience. This initial decision probably depends largely on circumstantial clues. On the basis of this decision, further data may be processed; but the data are probably processed more rapidly and effectively if they confirm the initial guess (cf. Bruner, 1957). Thus, if the experience is inferred to be internal, one may decide to disregard it totally (especially if in a situation of danger) or one may decide to follow it through (if one is more relaxed or if an experimenter has urged one to describe inner experiences). If the experience is inferred to be external, one usually reacts to it behaviorally by defining it more fully or by some derivative approach or avoidance response.

Sometimes, however, the initial decision is tentative, and the operator decides on a test procedure. The operator directs that more information be sampled from the external world, and the receptors are adjusted appropriately (Scheibel and Scheibel, 1962, Chapter 2, pp. 15–35). Because the operator has decided to increase the density of sensory input, it *infers* that the integrated impression which is now received depends on a denser sampling of sensory input, and is then prepared to make a second decision.

Many factors contribute to these decisions. The unique qualities of the sensory receptors are rarely duplicated by imagery, as reviewed in the early part of this report. Apparently, images usually are less vivid, smaller, and less clearly defined than percepts (Sheehan, 1966a; Brooks, 1967; Galton, 1883; Külpe, 1902). A percept will often have especially dark and clear edges with the contour lines strongly marked; this probably is mediated by the specific action of excitatory and inhibitory effects in the cells in the optic tract (Hubel and Weisel, 1962; Ratliff, 1965; Granit, 1955). Also, a percept usually shows considerable stability, because the physical event remains stable or shows predictable changes even as the observer changes his position in relation to it.

All these factors enter into the decision. An impression is received which includes both samplings from the external world and from the internal experiences and expectancies. If this impression seems not to relate to any external event—or if it clearly *is* related—no further processing is necessary. If further checking seems desirable, one may increase the density of external samplings, and reexamine the new impression. If a definitive decision still cannot be made, a further process of checking, resampling, and reevaluation may be in order, somewhat like the TOTE units of Miller, Galanter, and Pribram (1960). The urgency and importance of the decision will determine what level of certainty may be tolerated and when the decision process may be terminated.

The percept is simply the picture we build up of the world about us, but the image, while it depends more on needs, expectancies, and wishes, also is in close interrelationship to the external world. When we have been able to ascertain that a given impression shows adequate correlation with external events to satisfy our current needs, it is conventional to call it a "perception." When there is a disturbing lack of correspondence, the impression may be called an illusion, an image, a hallucination, or a dream. So remarkably effective is this decision process that it is commonly regarded as being nearly perfect. In fact, it is only in certain ambiguous situations that the decision is at all difficult to make. But from what we find to occur in these rare ambiguous situations, results which can be synthesized and investigated in the experimental laboratory, it may be possible to understand better the processes underlying all subjective experiences, whether they are classified as hallucinations, images, perceptions, or reality.

REFERENCES

Antrobus, J. S. Information theory and stimulus-independent thought. *British Journal of Psychology,* 1968, **59,** 423-430.

Antrobus, J. S., Coleman, R., & Singer, J. L. Signal-detection performance by subjects differing in predisposition to daydreaming. *Journal of Consulting Psychology,* 1967, **31,** 487-491.

Antrobus, J. S., Singer, J. L., & Greenberg, S. Studies in the stream of consciousness: experimental enhancement and suppression of spontaneous cognitive processes. *Perceptual and Motor Skills,* 1966, **23,** 399-417.

Attneave, F. Perception and related areas. In S. Koch (Ed.), *Psychology: A study of a science,* Vol. IV. New York: McGraw-Hill, 1962.

Barber, T. X. The after images of "hallucinated" and "imagined" colors. *Journal of Abnormal and Social Psychology,* 1959, **59,** 136-139.

Barber, T. X. Hypnotically hallucinated colors and their negative after images. *American Journal of Psychology,* 1964, **77,** 313-318.

Bartlett, F. C. *Remembering.* London: Cambridge University Press, 1932.

Bexton, W. H., Heron, W., & Scott, T. H. Effects of decreased variation in the sensory environment. *Canadian Journal of Psychology,* 1954, 8, 70-76.

Binet, A., & Féré, C. *Animal magnetism.* London: Kegan Paul, Trench, Trubner and Company, Ltd., 1891.

Brooks, L. R. Suppression of visualization by reading. *Quarterly Journal of Experimental Psychology,* 1967, 19, 289-299.

Bruner, J. S. On perceptual readiness. *Psychological Review,* 1957, 64, 123-152.

Crovitz, H. F. Flicker fusion measured in sensation vs. imagery. Presented at the 10th meeting of the Psychonomic Society, St. Louis, 1969.

Downey, J. E. An experiment on getting an afterimage from a mental image. *Psychological Review,* 1901, 8, 42-55.

Ellson, D. G. Hallucinations produced by sensory conditioning. *Journal of Experimental Psychology,* 1941, 28, 1-20.

Ellson, D. G. Critical conditions influencing sensory conditioning. *Journal of Experimental Psychology,* 1942, 31, 333-338.

Eriksen, C. W. Discrimination and learning without awareness: a methodological survey and evaluation. *Psychological Review,* 1960, 67, 279-300.

Erickson, M. H., & Erickson, E. M. The hypnotic induction of hallucinatory color vision followed by pseudo-images. *Journal of Experimental Psychology,* 1938, 22, 581-588.

Fisher, C. Dreams and perception. *Journal of American Psychoanalytic Association,* 1954, 3, 389-445.

Fisher, C., & Paul, I. H. The effect of subliminal visual stimulation on imagery and dreams: a validation study. *Journal of American Psychoanalytic Association,* 1959, 7, 35-83.

Fiss, H., Goldberg, F. H., & Klein, G. S. Effects of subliminal stimulation on imagery and discrimination. *Perceptual and Motor Skills,* 1963, 17, 31-44.

Galton, F. *Inquiries into the human faculty and its development.* London: MacMillan and Company, 1883.

Goldiamond, I. Indicators of Perception: I. Subliminal perception, subception, unconscious perception. *Psychological Bulletin,* 1958, 55, 373-411.

Granit, R. *Receptors and sensory perception.* New Haven: Yale University Press, 1955.

Green, D. M., & Swets, J. A. *Signal detection theory and psychophysics.* New York: Wiley, 1966.

Haber, R. N., & Haber, R, B. Eidetic imagery: I Frequency. *Perceptual and Motor Skills,* 1964, 19, 131-138.

Hebb, D. O. Concerning imagery. *Psychological Review,* 1968, 75, 466-477.

Hibler, F. W. An experimental investigation of negative after images of hallucinated color vision followed by pseudo-negative after images. *Journal of Experimental Psychology,* 1938, 22, 581-588.

Horowitz, M. The imagery of visual hallucinations. *Journal of Nervous and Mental Diseases,* 1964, 138, 513-523.

Horowitz, M. Visual imagery and cognitive organization. *American Journal of Psychiatry,* 1967, 123, 938-946.

Hubel, D. H., & Wiesel, T. N. Receptive fields, binocular interaction, and functional architecture in the cat's visual cortex. *Journal of Physiology,* 1962, 160, 106-154.

Jaensch, E. R. *Eidetic imagery.* London: Kegan Paul, Trench, Trubner and Company, Ltd., 1930.

Kelley, E. L. An experimental attempt to produce artificial chromaesthesia by the technique of the conditioned response. *Journal of Experimental Psychology,* 1934, 17, 315-341.

Klein, G. S., Spence, D. P., Holt, R. R., & Gourevitch, S. Cognition without awareness: subliminal influences upon conscious thought. *Journal of Abnormal and Social Psychology*, 1958, **57**, 255-266.

Klüver, H. *Mescal and mechanisms of hallucinations*. Chicago: University of Chicago Press, 1966.

Klüver, H. Studies on the eidetic type and on eidetic imagery. *Psychological Bulletin*, 1928, **25**, 66-104.

Külpe, O. Über die Objectivirung und Subjectivirung von Sinneseindrucken. *Philosophische Studien*, 1902, **19**, 508-556.

Leask, J., Haber, R. N., & Haber, R. B. Eidetic imagery in children. II: Longitudinal and experimental results, 1968. (Unpublished)

Leuba, C. Images as conditioned sensation. *Journal of Experimental Psychology*, 1940, **26**, 345-351.

Luria, A. R. *The mind of a mnemonist*. New York: Avon, 1968.

Malhotra, M. K. Signal after effects: An examination of Kohler's theory. *Acta Psychologica*, 1958, **14**, 161-198.

Miller, G. A., Galanter, E., & Pribram, K. H. *Plans and the structure of behavior*. New York: Holt, Rinehart and Winston, 1960.

Miller, J. W. The empty visual field in the laboratory and in the air. *Naval Research Reviews*. ONR, Washington, D. C., July, 1960.

Miller, R. J., Lundy, R. M., & Galbraith, G. G. The effects of the hypnotically induced hallucination of a color filter. Presented at the 10th meeting of the Psychonomic Society, St. Louis, 1969.

Neisser, U. *Cognitive psychology*. New York: Appleton, 1967.

Neisser, U. Visual imagery as process and as experience. In Antrobus, J. (Ed.) *Cognition and affect*. Boston: Little Brown, 1970.

Perky, C. W. An experimental study of imagination. *American Journal of Psychology*, 1910, **21**, 422-452.

Piaget, J. *Play, dreams and imitation in childhood*. New York: Norton, 1951.

Pötzl, O. The relationship between experimentally induced dream images and indirect vision. First published *Z. Neurol. Psychiat.*, 1917, **37**, 278-349. [Translated by Wolff, J., Rapaport, D., and Annin, S., *Psychological Issues*, **2** (whole No. 3), Monograph 7, 41-120]

Ratliff, F. *Mach bands: Quantitative studies on neural networks in the retina*. San Francisco: Holden Day, 1965.

Rosenthal, B. G., & Mele, H. The validity of hypnotically induced color hallucinations. *Journal of Abnormal and Social Psychology*, 1952, **47**, 700-704.

Saravay, S., & Pardes, H. Auditory elementary hallucinations in alcohol withdrawal psychosis. *Archives of General Psychiatry*, 1967, **16**, 652-658.

Scheibel, M. E., & Scheibel, A. B. Hallucinations and the brain stem reticular core. In West, L. J. (Ed.), *Hallucinations*. New York: Grune and Stratton, 1962.

Scripture, E. W. Measuring hallucinations. *Science*, 1896, **3**, 762-763.

Segal, S. J. Effect of thirst on Perky effect, *unpublished data*, 1965.

Segal, S. J. Patterns of response to thirst in an imaging task (Perky technique) as a function of cognitive style. *Journal of Personality*, 1968, **36**, 574-588. (a)

Segal, S. J. The Perky effect: Changes in reality judgments with changing methods of inquiry. *Psychonomic Science*, 1968, **12**, 393-394. (b)

Segal, S. J., & Fusella, V. Effect of images in six sense modalities on detection (d') of visual signal from noise, *Psychonomic Science*, in press, 1971.

Segal, S. J., & Fusella, V. Effects of imaging on signal-to-noise ratio with varying signal conditions. *British Journal of Psychology,* 1969, **60**, 459-464. (a)

Segal, S. J., & Fusella, V. Influence of imaged pictures and sounds on detection of auditory and visual signals. *Journal of Experimental Psychology,* 1970, **83**, 458-464. (a)

Segal, S. J., & Fusella, V. Processing of sensory input relative to a constructed image, 1970. Presented at 1970 meetings of Psychonomic Society, San Antonio. (b)

Segal, S. J., & Glicksman, M. Relaxation and the Perky effect: The influence of body position on judgments of imagery. *American Journal of Psychology,* 1967, **80**, 257-262.

Segal, S. J., & Gordon, P. The Perky effect revisited: Paradoxical threshold or signal detection error. *Perceptual and Motor Skills,* 1969, **28**, 791-797.

Segal, S. J., & Nathan, S. The Perky effect: Incorporation of an external stimulus into an imagery experience under placebo and control conditions. *Perceptual and Motor Skills,* 1964, **18**, 385-395.

Sheehan, P. W. Accuracy and vividness of visual images. *Perceptual and Motor Skills,* 1966, **23**, 391-398. (a)

Sheehan, P. W. Functional similarity of imaging to perceiving: individual differences in vividness of imagery. *Perceptual and Motor Skills,* Monograph Supplement, 1966, **6-V23**, 1011-1033. (b)

Shevrin, H., & Luborsky, L. The measurement of preconscious perception in dreams and images: an investigation of the Poetzl phenomenon. *Journal of Abnormal and Social Psychology,* 1958, **56**, 285-294.

Shurley, J. T. Mental imagery in profound sensory isolation. In West, L. J.(Ed.), *Hallucinations.* New York: Grune and Stratton, 1962.

Silverman, A. J., Cohen, S. I., Bressler, B., & Shmavonian, M. Hallucinations in sensory deprivation. In West, L. J.(Ed.), *Hallucinations,* New York: Grune and Stratton, 1962.

Silverman, L. Personal communication, 1966.

Singer, G., & Sheehan, P. W. The effect of demand characteristics on the figural after effect with real and imaged inducing figures. *American Journal of Psychology,* 1965, **78**, 96-101.

Stromeyer, C. F. III. Eidetikers, *Psychology Today,* 1970, **4**, 76–80.

Stromeyer, C. F. III, & Psotka, J. The detailed texture of eidetic images. *Nature,* 1970, **225**, 346-349.

Swets, J. A. Is there a sensory threshold? *Science,* 1961, **134**, 168-177.

Swets, J. A. *Signal detection and recognition by human observers: Contemporary readings.* New York: Wiley, 1964.

Underwood, H. W. The validity of hypnotically induced visual hallucinations. *Journal of Abnormal and Social Psychology,* 1960, **61**, 39-46.

West, L. J. A general theory of hallucinations and dreams. In West, L. J. (Ed.), *Hallucinations.* New York: Grune and Stratton, 1962.

Ziskind, E. An explanation of mental symptoms found in acute sensory deprivation: researches 1958-1963. *American Journal of Psychiatry,* 1965, **121**, 939-946.

Zuckerman, M. Hallucinations, reported sensations, and images. In Zubek, J. P. (Ed.), *Sensory Deprivation: Fifteen years of research.* New York: Appleton, 1969.

CHAPTER 6

IMAGERY AND "HALLUCINATIONS": EFFECTS OF LSD CONTRASTED WITH THE EFFECTS OF "HYPNOTIC" SUGGESTIONS[1]

Theodore Xenophon Barber

Vivid imagery, "hallucinations," and other alterations in visual perception are said to be produced by lysergic acid diethylamide (LSD) and also by suggestions given under hypnosis. Do similar processes or mechanisms underlie the imagery or hallucinations found in an LSD situation and those that are elicited by suggestions in a hypnotic situation?

The visual phenomena associated with LSD include changes in color perception, distortions, illusions, and vivid imagery or hallucinations; these can be related to physiologically based alterations that have occurred in the pupil, the lens, the intraocular fluid, the retina, and in other structures within the visual system. The hallucinations that are said to be produced by hypnotic suggestions are somewhat different, as will be explained more fully in this chapter.

I will look closely at the reports of vivid imagery or hallucinations which are proffered by some hypnotic subjects, and also by some control subjects, who have received suggestions to hallucinate. Two major questions will underlie this part of

[1] Work on this paper was supported by a research grant (MH-11521) from the National Institute of Mental Health, U.S. Public Health Service.

the discussion: Do suggestions to see an object that is not actually present produce reports of visual hallucinations when honest reports are explicitly demanded? Do these suggested hallucinations give rise to any observable or objective effects which are independent of the subjects' verbal reports?

In addition, I will try to determine whether the visual phenomena associated with LSD are functionally related to subjects' expectancies, or to explicit or implicit suggestions made to the subjects. Finally, I will consider what areas of fruitful research are suggested by the data that we have at present.

LSD, PSILOCYBIN, AND MESCALINE[2]

Before we focus on the effects of LSD, we should note that psilocybin and mescaline also produce similar effects.

LSD is usually given orally at doses of about 100 to 300 micrograms whereas psilocybin is usually given at a much larger dose (30,000 to 60,000 micrograms) and mescaline at a still larger dose (350,000 to 600,000 micrograms). At these common doses, subjects generally report that the subjective effects of LSD, psilocybin, and mescaline are very similar (Abramson, 1960; Hollister and Hartman, 1962; Isbell, 1959; Unger, 1963; Wolbach, Miner, and Isbell, 1962). Furthermore, when a subject becomes tolerant to one of these drugs, that is, when he requires larger and larger doses to experience the characteristic effects of the drug, he also becomes tolerant to the others (Balestrieri and Fontanari, 1959; Isbell, Wolbach, Wikler, and Miner, 1961). Although LSD, psilocybin, and mescaline produce very similar *subjective* effects, there are some objective differences in their mode of action. For example, at commonly administered doses, LSD and mescaline exert noticeable psychological and physiological effects over a period of 8 to 12 hours, whereas the action of psilocybin lasts only 3 to 4 hours. However, the important point that requires emphasis is that the similarities in the subjectively reported effects of LSD, psilocybin, and mescaline far outweigh the differences.[3]

[2] The first half of this paper, which pertains to LSD and related drugs, is based on material presented in more detail elsewhere (Barber, 1970).

[3] There are many other drugs that appear to produce at least some of the effects that are characteristic of LSD, psilocybin and mescaline. These include dimethyltryptamine (DMT), diethyltryptamine (DET), tetrahydrocannabinol (THC), and dimethoxymethylamphetamine (DOM, also known popularly as "STP") (Hollister, Macnicol, and Gillespie, 1969; Isbell, 1967; Isbell, Gorodetzsky, Jasinski, Claussen, Spulak, and Korte, 1967; Rosenberg, Isbell, Miner, and Logan, 1964; Snyder, Faillace, and Hollister, 1967; Snyder, Faillace, and Weingartner, 1968; Szara, Rockland, Rosenthal, and Handlon, 1966). Other drugs that may also produce some LSD-type effects have been reviewed by Farnsworth (1968), Hoffer and Osmond (1967), Hollister (1968), and Schultes (1969).

GENERAL EFFECTS OF LSD

Although the effects of LSD are often discussed as if they constituted an undifferentiated conglomerate, they can actually be differentiated into a series of distinguishable effects (Barber, 1970). These isolable effects of LSD include the following:

1. *Somatic—sympathetic effects.* These effects which are usually found within the first hour after ingestion of the drug and which are related to changes occurring in the autonomic nervous system include subjective reports of physical weakness, dizziness, restlessness, or difficulties in breathing, and objectively observable phenomena such as pupillary dilation and elevation in body temperature and blood pressure.

2. *Changes in "body image."* Subjects report that the body (or parts of the body, especially the limbs) feel strange—heavier or lighter, or changed in size, shape, or in relative proportions.

3. *Dreamy, detached feelings.* Subjects report that things are strange or distant, and they feel that they are observing the world in a dreamlike way. To an objective observer the subjects may appear to be in a state of reverie, fantasy, or introspection.

4. *Changes in perception of time.* Subjects almost always report a change in their perception of the passage of time and they typically judge a short period as a longer period.

5. *Changes in tactile sensitivity.* Subjects typically report that their fingers or extremities are numb or rubbery, and that objects feel different when they are touched.

6. *Changes in visual perception.* These visual effects, which will be discussed in detail below, include changes in color perception, illusions, distortions, and vivid imagery or hallucinations.

7. *Changes in audition, gustation, and olfaction.* Subjects characteristically report that music or other sounds have changed in quality, food tastes different (better or worse), and odors are more pronounced.

8. *Synesthesia.* Some subjects report that one sense modality affects another sense modality. For example, the visual forms which the subject perceives with eyes closed are altered whenever the music which is being played changes in tempo.

9. *Changes in moods, emotions, and cognitions.* Some individuals who have taken LSD do not show marked changes in moods, emotions, or cognitions.

However, most subjects who have taken this drug do show emotional and cognitive reactions. Some subjects become euphoric (and may move on to joy, bliss, or a "psychedelic" reaction), whereas others become anxious (and may move on to a panic reaction).

Although each of these nine effects of LSD is important in understanding the effects of this drug, in this chapter I will focus only on the changes in visual perception.

EFFECTS OF LSD ON VISUAL PERCEPTION

When subjects ingest LSD at usual doses (100–300 micrograms), almost all report some changes in the perception of colors, or in the size or form of objects, persons, or their own body (Fiddleman, 1961). These visual phenomena are among the most characteristic effects of LSD and have given this drug the name of "hallucinogen."

VISUAL EFFECTS WITH EYES CLOSED

When the eyes are closed, normal individuals perceive phosphenes (starlike objects and colors) in their visual field. When subjects who have received LSD (or psilocybin or mescaline) close their eyes in a dark room, they typically report that the phosphenes are more vivid than those perceived normally; in fact, some subjects report that the luminescent lights, colors, and patterns change into formed structures such as gemlike or architectural-like objects (Cohen, 1968, pp. 22-24; Ditman, Moss, Forgy, Zunin, Lynch, and Funk, 1969; Huxley, 1954). In most instances, the subjects continue to see these colorful patterns or structures when they open their eyes in a dark room. However, when the lights are turned on in the room, almost all subjects report that the visual phenomena have become very faint or have disappeared (Pahnke and Richards, 1966).

Experiments by Knoll and his associates seem to corroborate the reports that LSD (and psilocybin and mescaline) augment the phosphene phenomenon. First, these investigators showed that complexly patterned phosphenes can be evoked by electrical stimulation of the brain with pulses ranging in frequency from 1 to 30 cps (Knoll and Kugler, 1959). Then, in a second experiment (Knoll, Kugler, Hofer, and Lawder, 1963), they showed that under LSD (and psilocybin and mescaline) a greater number of complexly patterned phosphenes are elicited by the electrical stimulation and there is an increase in the vividness of these phosphenes.

VISUAL EFFECTS WITH EYES OPEN

Within an hour or two after taking LSD, and usually continuing in a wavelike manner for several hours, many subjects report that colors seem brighter or more intense or vivid. Also, subjects typically report that they can see rainbowlike colors, colored patterns, or halos at the edges of objects or on the wall and that colored afterimages persist longer than usual (Bercel, Travis, Olinger, and Dreikurs, 1956; Masters and Huston, 1966, pp. 152–153).

Perception of depth and perspective are also altered. A change in depth relations is indicated by subjects' reports that two-dimensional objects at times seem to be three-dimensional (Kieffer and Moritz, 1968). The outlines or contours of objects, especially the edges, appear to become sharper (Kluver, 1966). Corridors often appear longer than usual and objects at times seem to fluctuate in distance (Andersen and Rawnsley, 1954; Hoffer and Osmond, 1967, p. 112). Also common is a magnification of detail, which may be related to the changes in contours, perspective, or simultaneous contrast (Rodin and Luby, 1966). The constancies of perception are no longer constant—a typical report is, "As I moved my hand toward me, it increased in size." These changes in depth perception and in the constancies of perception are clearly noted when the subject looks in a mirror; practically all subjects who have taken LSD report that their own image in a mirror or the image of another person appears distorted in some way (Masters and Huston, 1966, p. 83).

Other common visual phenomena associated with LSD include alterations in the size or shapes of objects. Parts of one's own body, or the features of another person, or objects in the room may be perceived as changed in some way if not markedly distorted. Also, at higher doses of LSD (above 350 micrograms), subjects often report apparent undulations or movements of surfaces; a piece of paper may seem to be making wavelike motions and the wall may seem to ripple in and out (Ditman *et al.*, 1969; Hoffer and Osmond, 1967, pp. 113–114).

Experimental studies tend to corroborate the subjects' reports that the visual world has changed. Hartman and Hollister (1963) demonstrated that colored afterimages and also the subjective colors elicited by flicker were increased by LSD (and also by psilocybin and mescaline). The same investigators also showed that the duration of afterimages was prolonged by psilocybin, although the effect was not significant for LSD and mescaline. Along similar lines, Keeler (1965) demonstrated, under double-blind conditions, that psilocybin significantly changed an objective measure of afterimage perception.

LSD augments the variability in judging the size of test objects (Weckowicz, 1959) and increases the degree of displacement of the vertical that is produced by tilting the body (Liebert, Wapner, and Werner, 1957). Edwards and Cohen (1961) found that the Mueller-Lyer illusion was slightly enhanced under LSD and the same investigators showed that constancy decreased when the standard object was nearby (30 centimeters away) but not when it was further away (180 centimeters).

VISUAL EFFECTS AS A FUNCTION OF SUBJECTS'
NORMAL VISUAL IMAGERY

Practically all subjects who have received a moderate dose of LSD (100–300 micrograms) report some changes in visual perception. However, as compared to individuals with ordinary visual imagery, individuals with exceptionally strong visual imagery (who normally project visual images in front of their eyes) report a greater number of more intense visual effects with LSD (Brown, 1968; Shryne and Brown, 1965). The subjects' visual imagery abilities interact with the drug dose to affect the visual manifestations; that is, subjects with weak imagery require a higher dose of LSD to report as many or as intense visual effects as those with strong imagery.

VISUAL EFFECTS AS A FUNCTION OF DOSE

A relationship between the drug dose and the number and intensity of the visual effects is difficult to demonstrate when comparisons are made among subjects (interindividual comparisons) (Klee, Bertino, Weintraub, and Callaway, 1961). Subjects differ in response to the same dose. Also, two subjects may report very similar visual effects even though one receives a high dose and the other a low dose. Different responses to the same dose may be due to differences among subjects in ability to detoxify and excrete the drug. Different responses to the same dose may also be related to differences among subjects in normal visual imagery abilities, in personality characteristics, and in motivations, expectancies, and attitudes toward the situation.

Although a dose-response relationship is difficult to demonstrate when interindividual comparisons are made, such a relationship can be clearly demonstrated when the *same* subject receives various doses of LSD (intraindividual comparisons). Any one subject will tend to report a greater number of more intense visual effects with increasingly higher doses of LSD (Abramson, Kornetsky, Jarvik, Kaufman, and Ferguson, 1955; Isbell, Belleville, Fraser, Wikler, and Logan, 1956; Klee *et al.*, 1961).

This important relationship, between the dose of LSD and the number and intensity of the visual effects, was clearly demonstrated in an experiment by Klee *et al.* (1961). In this experiment, 12 subjects, seen together as a group, were given LSD in 3 sessions at doses around 70, 140, and 280 micrograms, and then were given LSD again in 3 additional sessions at doses around 280, 560, and 1120 micrograms. A latin square design was used to counterbalance the doses and the experiment was double-blind (neither the subjects nor three medical observers knew which dose of LSD was being used). There was perfect agreement among the three observers as to the dose received by any one subject over three sessions; that is, the medical observers were able to tell which of the three doses each subject had received. For any one subject, the number and intensity of the visual effects clearly increased with increasingly higher doses of LSD up to the highest dose (around 1120 micrograms). (At the highest dose, confusion and disorientation were common.)

VISUAL EFFECTS, EXPECTANCY, AND SUGGESTIONS

As can be surmised from the study by Klee *et al.* described above, the visual effects of LSD appear to be more closely related to the drug dose than to the subjects' expectancies or to suggestions which are explicit or implicit in the experimental situation. Supporting data for this supposition, that expectancies and suggestions, at best, play only a minor role in producing the visual effects, have been presented by Ditman *et al.* (1969), Levis and Mehlman (1964), Fogel and Hoffer (1962), and Johnson (1968).

In the investigation by Ditman *et al.* (1969), 1 of the following 3 drugs were administered in randomized order and under double-blind conditions to 99 alcoholics: 75 milligrams of methylphenidate (Ritalin), which is usually categorized as a mild stimulant; 75 milligrams of chlordiazepoxide (Librium), which acts as a tranquilizer; or 200 micrograms of LSD. All subjects were told that they were receiving LSD and were treated as if they had received LSD. A major question that the study was designed to answer was: Would drugs, thought by the subjects to be LSD, produce the visual effects that have been associated with LSD, when the situation and the subjects' expectancies remain constant, although the actual drug administered varied? Following the drug session, all subjects checked a series of items which pertained to drug experiences. LSD far outranked the other two drugs in enhancing the phosphene phenomenon ("With my eyes closed I saw multicolored moving designs"), in affecting color perception ("Colors seemed brighter"), and in producing visual distortions, illusions, or hallucinations ("Solid objects changed their shapes and even disappeared," "Objects seemed to glow around the edges," and "Other people's faces seemed to become changing masks").

In a double-blind experiment (Levis and Mehlman, 1964), 15 subjects were given a placebo and another 15 subjects were given mescaline (350,000 micrograms). The subjects were divided into 3 groups, each group containing 5 placebo subjects and 5 mescaline subjects. One of the 3 groups was not given suggestions as to what to expect. The other 2 groups received a list of written statements suggesting what to expect from the drug. For instance, subjects in one group were told that they would experience visual illusions, and subjects in the other group were told that they would not experience visual illusions. The suggestions did *not* exert a significant effect on the visual phenomena produced by mescaline. Regardless of the suggestions, subjects receiving mescaline, but not those receiving the placebo, reported visual hallucinations (with eyes closed) and visual illusions and distortions (with eyes open).

Fogel and Hoffer (1962) attempted to reverse the visual effects of LSD by suggestions given under hypnosis. The subject in this study had taken 100 micrograms of LSD and was reporting visual phenomena; for instance, she stated that the face of the experimenter was altered in appearance. At this point, a hypnotic induction procedure was administered and the subject was given the suggestion that on opening her eyes everything would look normal. The subject stated that although the experimenter's face now looked more normal it still remained somewhat distorted. Although Fogel and Hoffer concluded that hypnotic suggestions negated the visual effects of LSD, a more justifiable conclusion is that hypnotic suggestions, at best, reduced but did not eliminate the visual changes produced by LSD.

Johnson (1968) showed that the visual effects of LSD are elicited when expectancies and suggestions are minimized, that is, when the subjects do not know that they have received LSD. Johnson administered 500 or more micrograms of LSD to one group of alcoholics and a combination of sodium amytal with methamphetamine to another group. The patients did not know that they were receiving LSD. The patients receiving LSD, but not those receiving sodium amytal with methamphetamine, reported the characteristic distortions and illusions which have been associated with LSD.

VISUAL EFFECTS AND HALLUCINATIONS

The discussion up to this point can be summarized as follows. When LSD (or mescaline or psilocybin) is taken at the doses which are commonly used in experimental studies, and the subject's eyes are closed, subjects typically report that they perceive vivid colors, patterns, and, at times, formed objects. Also, when the subjects' eyes are open, they report some alteration in visual perception such as changes in the color and form of objects. These visual phenomena which increase in number and in intensity in any one subject as the drug dose is increased and which are affected only to a minor degree by expectancies and suggestions have been commonly subsumed under the term "visual hallucination," and the drugs have been labeled as "hallucinogens." Is the term "hallucination" applicable?

The term visual hallucination, as used by different investigators, subsumes at least 4 dimensions: (a) the complexity of the phenomena which the subject reports (the visual phenomena can vary in complexity from simple lights or colors to completely formed persons or objects); (b) whether the subject's eyes are closed or open when he reports that he perceives the phenomena; (c) whether the subject reports that he perceives the phenomena "out there" or in his imagination or "mind's eye"; (d) the degree to which the subject believes that the things he perceives actually have an independent existence, are actually out there.

If the term hallucination is used strictly to refer to the extreme end of each of the four dimensions, it is clear that LSD (and psilocybin and mescaline) rarely produce hallucinations. That is, subjects who have ingested one of these drugs very rarely report, when their eyes are open, that they perceive formed persons or objects which they believe are actually out there (Cohen, 1967). Although complex, formed objects are at times reported, this almost always occurs only when the subjects' eyes are closed. Also, whenever formed objects are reported (either with eyes opened or closed), the subjects are practically always aware that the visual effects are due to the drug and are not actually out there. Very few subjects who have taken LSD report perceiving formed objects which they believe are actually out there. In these rare cases the subjects have almost always taken a high, toxic dose of the drug, and are confused and disoriented (Cohen, 1967, p. 52).

On the other hand, hallucinations can be said to be quite common with LSD provided that the term hallucination is used to refer either to (a) the subject's report (when his eyes are open) that he perceives lines, patterns, or colors out there (which he knows are not actually out there), or to (b) the subject's report (when his eyes are closed) that he perceives complex, formed objects in his visual field.

PHYSIOLOGICAL BASIS OF THE LSD
VISUAL PHENOMENA

LSD becomes highly concentrated in the visual system. For instance, as compared to its concentration in the cortex, cerebellum, and midbrain, the concentration of LSD in the iris is 18 times as high and its concentration in the optic chiasma and lateral geniculate nucleus of the visual system is 2 to 6 times as high (Snyder and Reivich, 1966).

The visual phenomena that follow ingestion of LSD appear to be correlated with physiological changes that occur throughout the entire visual system, extending from the pupil, lens, and retina, on through the lateral geniculates and the occipital cortex. I will now trace the physiological changes that occur in various structures within the eyeball (pupil, lens, intraocular fluid, and retina), the possible relations between the LSD visual phenomena and entoptic phenomena, and the relation of the visual phenomena to physiological changes that have occurred at higher levels of the visual system.

PUPIL

LSD, psilocybin, and mescaline produce an enlarged pupil (mydriasis). Since dilation of the pupil allows more light to stimulate the retina, reduces the depth of focus, and maximizes the effects of spherical, chromatic, and other aberrations, it may play a role in producing some of the visual effects that are associated with these drugs. For instance, it may be related to the reports, proffered by some subjects who have taken LSD, that their vision is blurred, they find it difficult to focus their eyes, and they feel as if there is too much light. Furthermore, since the pupillary dilation maximizes chromatic aberrations, it may give rise to the "rainbow effect" (the perception of a series of rainbowlike colors at the edges of objects) which is reported by some subjects who have taken LSD.

Although the mydriasis produced by LSD, psilocybin, and mescaline may give rise to blurring, difficulties in focusing, and possibly the rainbow effect, it is not important in producing the other visual effects such as the illusions and distortions, that are commonly associated with these drugs. In a relevant experiment (Bertino, Klee, Collier, and Weintraub, 1960), subjects first received a sympathetic blocking agent (dibenzyline) and then ingested LSD. Although dibenzyline blocked the pupillary dilation produced by LSD, the subjects still manifested most of the visual distortions and illusions which are characteristically found with LSD.

CILIARY MUSCLE AND LENS

LSD affects the ciliary muscle, producing partial paralysis of the accommodation mechanism (Payne, 1965). Since the adjustment of the lens for various distances (accommodation) is due to contraction of the ciliary muscle (resulting in relaxation of the lens zonules and an increase in the lens thickness), the physiological effect of LSD on the ciliary muscle may play a role in producing the distortions of spatial perception. For example, these changes in the functioning of the lens may give rise to the LSD subjects' reports that objects appear larger or smaller than normal (Heaton, 1968, pp. 138–139).

PRESSURE OF THE INTRAOCULAR FLUID

By exerting pressure on the closed eyeballs, normal individuals (who have not taken a drug) can increase the vividness of the phosphenes. In fact, continuous pressure on the eyeballs at times transforms the starlike objects and luminescent colors into gemlike objects or architectural-like structures.

LSD tends to produce a significant rise in intraocular pressure (Holliday and Sigurdson, 1965). Since phosphenes may be due, in part, to pressure on the retina by the fluids of the eyeball (Ladd-Franklin, 1927), the elevated intraocular pressure may be functionally related to the LSD subject's report that the luminescent dots and colored patterns which he perceives with closed eyes are more vivid than normal or are transformed into gemlike objects or architectural-like structures.

The elevated intraocular pressure may also be related to the rainbow effect that is reported by some subjects who have ingested LSD. This possibility is suggested by the fact that whenever a patient reports that he perceives colored halos around lights the trained ophthalmologist immediately suspects that the pressure in the patient's eyeball may be abnormally high (Adler, 1962, p. 8).

ENTOPTIC PHENOMENA

Every normal individual is able to see some structures within his own eyeball. These entoptic phenomena (visual phenomena that have their seat within the eyeball) include, for example, the small hazy spots, specks, and hairlike objects that drift across the field of vision with movements of the eyes. These "spots before the eyes" are due to floating impurities in the vitreous humor, such as red blood cells, which cast shadows on the retina and are seen as hovering in space (White and Levatin, 1962).

Marshall (1937) hypothesized that mescaline (and presumably LSD and psilocybin) reduce "the threshold of the visual centres for the perception of low intensities of light-energy so that, with closed eyes or in the dark such almost infinitesimal [entoptic] stimuli . . . are in some measure perceived." Kluver (1966) pointed out that subjects who have taken mescaline typically perceive 3 types of forms when their eyes are closed: spiral-like forms; tunnel- or funnel-like forms; and grating- or lattice-type forms. Kluver hypothesized that mescaline gives rise to these 3 types of forms by enhancing the subject's sensitivity to entoptic phenomena; for instance, the spiral-like forms could be due to entoptic observation of the superficial retinal blood vessels, and the grating- or lattice-type forms could be due to entoptic observation of the regular arrangement of the rods and cones.

Further studies are needed to test the hypothesis that LSD (and psilocybin and mescaline) lower the threshold for the perception of entoptic phenomena. If the hypothesis is valid, we would have an explanation of the mechanisms which underlie some of the visual effects that are associated with these drugs.

RETINA

It appears that LSD may exert a direct effect on the retina which is independent of its effects on higher levels of the visual system.

Burian, Fleming, and Featherstone (1958) presented subthreshold light flashes to rabbits that were immobilized in a light-tight box. The subliminal stimuli were presented to one group of animals under a control condition and to another group under LSD. The voltage on the electroretinogram produced by the subthreshold stimuli was significantly greater under LSD as compared to the control condition.

Working with humans, Krill, Wieland, and Ostfeld (1960) and Rodin and Luby (1966) found that the beta wave of the electroretinogram increased in amplitude with LSD. Krill, Alpert, and Ostfeld (1963) also showed that the effect on the beta wave is most likely due to a direct action of LSD on the retina (not due to centrifugal influences on the retina from higher centers). These investigators gave LSD to two subjects with total optic nerve atrophy but with functioning retina. Since the beta wave amplitude increased in these subjects in the same way as in normal subjects, it appears that LSD exerts a direct effect on the retina.

Edwards and Cohen (1966) attempted to determine whether the locus of misperception of size with LSD is peripheral or at higher levels of the visual system. They compared subjects' misperception of size when two stimuli are presented simultaneously to both eyes and also independently to the two eyes. Edwards and Cohen reasoned that if the misperception occurs at the retinal level, the two situations should produce the same degree of misperception, that is, higher levels of the visual system should receive information from the retina which was already distorted. Since the two situations produced an equal degree of misperception of size, Edwards and Cohen concluded that the locus of the LSD effect on perception was peripheral, presumably retinal, rather than at higher levels of the visual system.

Studies by Apter and Pfeiffer (1957), Short (1958), and Jacobson and Gestring (1959), which attempted to demonstrate a direct effect of LSD on the retina, led to equivocal results.

Apter and Pfeiffer (1957) observed spontaneous retinal potentials in anesthetized cats 10 minutes after intraperitoneal injection of 100 micrograms of LSD. Two sets of data indicated that the potentials originated in the retina and were not due to centrifugal fibers. (a) The spontaneous potentials were first picked up in the retina and then in the optic nerve. (b) When the optic nerve was cut while the spontaneous potentials were being recorded, the spikes in the occipital cortex and those in the proximal stump of the optic nerve disappeared, while those in the distal stump of the optic nerve and those in the retina persisted. However, Short (1958) failed to confirm these results. In a brief note, Short reported that no significant increase in spontaneous potentials was found in the cat electroretinogram following injections of LSD over a wide range of doses.

Jacobson and Gestring (1959) reported that large doses of LSD (more than 50 micrograms per kilogram of body weight) produced spontaneous retinal potentials in 40% of their animals (cats). However, in contradistinction to the results presented by Apter and Pfeiffer (1957), the spontaneous retinal potentials were no longer observed when the optic nerve was cut. To explain their results, Jacobson and Gestring (1959) hypothesized the existence of an inhibitory center at a higher level of the nervous system which affects the electrical activity of the retina through centrifugal fibers.

In brief, it appears that LSD may effect the retina directly, and also indirectly through an effect on obscure centrifugal pathways.

HIGHER LEVELS OF THE VISUAL SYSTEM

The visual phenomena associated with LSD (and with psilocybin and mescaline) are not solely due to physiological effects produced by these drugs on structures within the eyeball (the pupil, the lens, the intraocular fluid, and the retina). Higher levels of the visual system are also involved. Reciprocal interactions and feedback mechanisms appear to integrate all levels of the visual system. Activity in the retina and in other structures within the eyeball appears to be integrated with activity at higher levels of the visual system. Consequently, the visual phenomena associated with LSD (and with psilocybin and mescaline) are probably related to the effects of these drugs on the total visual system and are not simply due to their effects on localized anatomical areas such as the retina.

Jacobson and Gestring (1959) could explain their results concerning retinal activity with LSD only by positing a higher center that exerts an inhibitory effect on retinal functions. Krill *et al.* (1963) also presented data which indicated that higher centers are involved. These investigators administered LSD to individuals who were blind, but who still perceived spots, flickers of light, or colors in their visual field. LSD increased the frequency and intensity of the spots, lights, and colors in these blind individuals. Since the retina was not functioning in these subjects, it appears that a normal retina is not necessary for the occurrence of at least some of the visual effects associated with LSD, and that higher levels of the visual system must also play a role in producing these phenomena. In fact, some of the visual phenomena associated with these drugs may be related to the simple noncolored forms that are commonly obtained by stimulation of Area 17 of the occipital lobe, to the complex and colored visual phenomena that are at times elicited by stimulation of the temporal lobe, and to the simple and complex visual phenomena that can be produced by stimulation of other areas of the visual system such as the optic radiations, optic tract, optic chiasma, or optic nerve (Penfield, 1958; Weinberger and Grant, 1940).

From the study of the effects of LSD on blind individuals, Krill *et al.* (1963) concluded that the concept of "localization" may be misleading in attempting to comprehend the visual phenomena associated with LSD. This cogent conclusion is in line with that of Purpura (1967, pp. 158–185) who stated that, "Perceptual disturbances produced by LSD obviously involve more than the neural machinery comprising the classical visual pathways. Insofar as activation of a considerable proportion of the neuraxis from mesencephalon to forebrain occurs as a consequence of a particular visual stimulus, it is well to keep in mind the involvement of diffusely organized nonspecific projection systems in the overt manifestations of the drug."

We will look at the effects of LSD on vision once again at the end of this paper after we have discussed the visual hallucinations that are said to be produced by suggestions.

SUGGESTIONS, HYPNOTIC INDUCTION,
AND VISUAL HALLUCINATION

It has been claimed that suggestions to hallucinate are effective in producing visual hallucinations in many subjects who have been exposed to a hypnotic induction procedure and in some control subjects who have not been exposed to a hypnotic induction (Barber, 1969a; Estabrooks, 1943; Hilgard, 1965; Weitzenhoffer, 1953). Let us first denote the three critical terms in this assertion, namely "suggestions to hallucinate," "hypnotic induction procedure," and "visual hallucination."

Statements such as, "In a moment you will see a [specified object] in the room," are labeled as suggestions to hallucinate when they are given in a situation in which the object is not actually present.

The term hypnotic induction refers to various procedures. For example, the subject may be instructed to keep his gaze on a swinging pendulum or a blinking light, he may be told that he is becoming progressively more and more relaxed, or he may be told repeatedly that he is becoming drowsy, sleepy, and is entering a hypnotic state. These and other procedures are termed hypnotic inductions because they include one common element: they explicitly or implicitly suggest to the subject that he is now entering a unique or different state (a hypnotic or trance state) in which he will be able to have unique or different experiences.

The term visual hallucination commonly refers to the subject's report that he clearly saw the suggested object out there. A few subjects who report that they clearly see the suggested object also report that they believe it is actually out there, and a few behave overtly as if it is actually out there. For example, they "pet" a suggested cat. I will henceforth use the term visual hallucination as is commonly done when referring to the subject's report that he clearly sees the suggested object out there, regardless of whether or not he believes or acts as if what he sees has an independent existence.

In discussing the suggested visual hallucination we can easily fall into a quagmire. Subjects participating in any experiment, and especially subjects participating in an experiment which involves suggestions, may proffer verbal reports which are not in line with their private experiences in order to fulfill the desires of the experimenter or to be "good" subjects (Barber, 1962, 1967 pp. 444–480; Barber and Silver, 1968a, 1968b; Rosenthal, 1968). Specifically, when subjects are instructed to see an object (which is not actually present) they may state that they see it in order to meet the explicit experimental demands. This important consideration must be kept in mind while examining the relevant data.

Four recent studies (Barber and Calverley, 1964; Barber, Spanos, and Merritt, 1970; Bowers, 1967; Spanos and Barber, 1968) attempted to specify the parameters of the suggested visual hallucination. In each of these studies subjects were given suggestions worded as follows: "I want you to look at your lap and to see a cat sitting there. Keep looking at the cat until I tell you to stop." Afterwards the subject checked a rating scale pertaining to the vividness of the suggested hallucination; for example, on the rating scale they checked, "Saw the cat clearly," "Saw a vague impression of the cat," and "Did not see the cat." Some of the subjects in these experiments received the suggestion to hallucinate under a control condition (without any special preliminaries), others received the same suggestion after they had received a hypnotic induction procedure, and still others were given the suggestion after they had received special instructions designed to elicit maximal performance (task-motivational instructions). Also, prior to completing the rating scale pertaining to the vividness of the suggested hallucination, some of the subjects were and others were not exposed to explicit demands for honesty. The results of these experiments can be briefly summarized as follows:

1. *Quite a few subjects reported a visual hallucination when it was suggested under the control condition.* In three of the experiments cited above (Barber and Calverley, 1964; Bowers, 1967; Spanos and Barber, 1968) unselected subjects (college students and nursing students) were given the suggestion to see the cat without any special preliminaries (control condition). From 20% to 33% of the subjects in these control groups reported that they clearly saw the suggested object.

In one of these experiments (Spanos and Barber, 1968) subjects in the control group were told by a co-experimenter that honest reports were desired and that they should not state they saw the object simply because they thought it would please the experimenter. This demand for honesty was made toward the end of the experiment and immediately before the subject rated the vividness of the suggested hallucination. The demand for honesty did not significantly affect the reports of visual hallucinations. Regardless of whether or not honesty was demanded, from 20% to 33% of the control subjects reported that they clearly saw the suggested object.

2. *When honesty was not demanded, more "task-motivated" subjects than control subjects reported visual hallucinations. However, when honesty was demanded once at the end of the experiment, task-motivational instructions did not raise reports of visual hallucinations above the control level.* In 3 of the experiments cited above (Barber and Calverley, 1964; Bowers, 1967; Spanos and

Barber, 1968), some of the subjects were given task-motivational instructions before they received the suggestions to hallucinate. In these task-motivational instructions, the subjects were told that they could perform well on the hallucination task if they tried to "control their mind" and if they took the attitude that it was easy to perform. About 50% of these task-motivated subjects reported that they clearly saw the suggested object. However, when honesty was explicitly demanded of these task-motivated subjects, reports of visual hallucinations were no greater than under the control condition (Barber, 1969b; Bowers, 1967; Spanos and Barber, 1968).

3. *When honesty was not demanded, and also when honesty was demanded only once toward the end of the experiment, more hypnotic subjects than control subjects reported visual hallucinations. However, when honesty was demanded at the beginning of the experiment and several times during the experiment, a hypnotic induction procedure did not raise reports of visual hallucinations above the control level.* When honesty was not demanded, from 53% to 65% of the subjects who had been exposed to a hypnotic induction procedure reported that they clearly saw the suggested object (Barber and Calverley, 1964; Spanos and Barber, 1968). When honesty was demanded once toward the end of the experiment, immediately before the subjects completed the rating scale, 40% of the hypnotic subjects reported a visual hallucination (Spanos and Barber, 1968). However, when subjects were told at the very beginning of the experiment, and several times during the experiment, that complete honesty was desired, the percentage of subjects (18%) under the hypnotic induction condition reporting a visual hallucination was no greater than under the control condition (Barber, *et al.,* 1970).

These results can be compressed as follows: When honesty is demanded once toward the end of the experiment, at least 20% of subjects in a control group and in a task-motivated group report that they clearly saw a suggested object. When honesty is demanded at the beginning of the experiment and several times during the experiment, about 20% of the subjects who have received a hypnotic induction procedure report that they clearly saw a suggested object.

How would we interpret these results? Unfortunately, none of the studies cited above attempted to determine what the subjects meant when they reported that they clearly saw the suggested object. Did some subjects mean that they saw it in the same way that they see an actual object? Did other subjects mean to say that they saw it in the same way they see an afterimage? Did other subjects mean that they clearly saw it in their "mind's eye"? Until such questions are answered, the results cannot be clearly interpreted.

Further studies in this area may find that at least some subjects who state that they clearly see the suggested object are saying that they see it clearly or vividly imagine it in their mind's eye. A neglected study by Sidis (1906) is relevant here. Sidis found that when subjects participated in hypnotic training sessions they reported that the suggested object became increasingly more vivid. However, Sidis also presented data indicating that the trained hypnotic subjects had not learned to hallucinate more proficiently; on the contrary, it appeared that the trained subjects had learned to give the type of verbal reports that were desired and expected. Sidis observed that the subjects gave more emphatic reports concerning the clarity and reality of the suggested object as they participated in more and more hypnotic sessions even though they showed as many signs of deep trance in the first session as in the later sessions. He interpreted these data as indicating that the subjects vividly imagined in the same way in all sessions but had learned, after participating in a number of hypnotic training sessions, that emphatic verbal reports concerning the clarity and lifelike qualities of the suggested object were desired and expected.

Goldiamond and Malpass (1961) also presented data indicating that the reports of hypnotic subjects with respect to visual hallucinations can be rather easily manipulated experimentally. Working with nonhypnotic subjects, Dobie (1959) demonstrated that nonverbal reinforcement procedures are effective in inducing a substantial proportion of normal individuals to testify that they see objects that are not present. Along related lines, Murphy and Myers (1962) found that reports of visual hallucinations in a pseudosensory-deprivation situation (remaining in the dark for only 10 minutes) can be augmented and also inhibited by simple preexperimental instructions to the effect that such hallucinations are normal and desirable or abnormal and undesirable.

Fisher (1962, pp. 109–126) hypothesized that subjects participating in hypnotic experiments "learn the intended thoroughness of hallucinations just as they learn other behavioral consistencies—from reinforcements, approvals, and disapprovals in the context of the situation." Careful research is needed to confirm Sidis' results and to test Fisher's related hypothesis. It may be that 3 factors are involved in the suggested hallucination: (a) the subject's normal ability to image or to imagine; (b) the removal of inhibiting factors so that the subject can utilize his normal abilities maximally; (c) the reinforcement given to the subject for reporting that the suggested object is clear and realistic. The reinforcement may produce more and more emphatic *reports* while the subject's imagery, or imagining, or hallucinating remains constant.

OBJECTIVE CONCOMITANTS OF SUGGESTED HALLUCINATIONS

A series of investigators have looked at the suggested visual hallucination to try to determine whether there are any objectively measurable effects that are correlated with the subject's report that he clearly sees the suggested object. Objective concomitants of suggested visual hallucinations have been assessed by measuring pupil dilation and contraction, negative afterimages, distortions produced by optical illusions, and nystagmus. Let us look at the studies pertaining to each of these measures.

PUPIL DILATION AND CONTRACTION

The pupil of the eye contracts when stimulated by light and dilates in darkness. When subjects are given suggestions to visualize vividly or to hallucinate a bright light, do they show pupillary contraction? Also, when subjects are given suggestions to visualize vividly or to hallucinate total darkness, do they show pupillary dilation?

Lundholm (1932) administered a hypnotic induction procedure to selected hypnotizable subjects and suggested that they were being stimulated by a very bright light. Although the subjects testified that they clearly saw the suggested light, none showed observable contraction of the pupil.

In a recent experiment, which is not yet published, Nicholas Spanos and I used a modern, automatic pupillometer[4] to measure pupil size accurately in two groups of subjects—a group exposed to a hypnotic induction procedure and a control group. Subjects in both groups were instructed individually to visualize vividly that the room was totally dark. Also, the room was made totally dark and subjects in both groups were instructed to visualize vividly a bright light in the room. Although some of the subjects in both groups testified that they could vividly visualize both the totally dark room and the bright light in the room, none showed clear-cut pupillary dilation when visualizing total darkness or unambiguous pupillary contraction when visualizing the bright light. The size of the pupils varied continuously during the experiment and it appeared that pupillary dilation and contraction were closely related to such factors as "trying to carry out instructions," "mental effort," or "concentration" rather than to "visualizing" per se.

NEGATIVE AFTERIMAGES

Introductory texts in psychology and physiology characteristically describe the negative afterimage phenomenon as follows. If a person with normal color vision fixates on a yellow surface for about 30 seconds and then looks at a neutral (gray or white) surface, he will see a blue afterimage; and if he fixates on a green surface and then looks at a neutral surface, he will see a red afterimage. Also, vice versa, fixation on a blue surface yields a yellow afterimage and fixation on a red surface gives rise to a green afterimage.

---

[4]We are indebted to the Polymetric Company of Hoboken, New Jersey, for the loan of the Pupillometer System, Model V-1165-IR.

Do suggested or hallucinated colors give rise to negative afterimages in the same way as actual colors? Working with selected "good" hypnotic subjects, Erickson and Erickson (1938) and Rosenthal and Mele (1952) reported that "hallucinated colors" gave rise to appropriate negative afterimages in a substantial proportion of subjects. An experiment by Barber (1959) included a group of selected good hypnotic subjects who were exposed to a hypnotic induction procedure and a group of unselected control subjects. Both groups were given suggestions to hallucinate the primary colors. Some subjects in both the hypnotic group and the control group reported that the hallucinated colors gave rise to negative afterimages. When interviewed postexperimentally, almost all of the subjects participating in the experiments of Erickson and Erickson, Rosenthal and Mele, and Barber denied that they had prior knowledge of the negative afterimage phenomenon.[5]

The conclusion indicated by the three studies described above, namely, that suggested or hallucinated colors give rise to negative afterimages, cannot be viewed as firmly established (Barber, 1964). Dorcus (1937), Naruse (1962, pp. 37–55), Elsea (1961), and other investigators failed to find any hypnotic subjects who reported negative afterimages to hallucinated colors. Sidis (1906) found that hypnotic subjects never claimed that hallucinated colors gave rise to negative afterimages when they were unacquainted with the negative afterimage phenomenon; however, they always reported such afterimages after this phenomenon had been carefully explained to them. Hibler (1935, 1940) found that the afterimages reported by hypnotic subjects varied with their preconceptions concerning the afterimage phenomenon. For instance, prior to the formal experiment, Hibler's subjects A, B, and C believed that the afterimage of blue was blue, orange, and yellow, respectively. When exposed to a hypnotic induction procedure and to suggestions to hallucinate blue, subjects A, B, and C testified, in harmony with their preconceptions, that the hallucinated blue gave rise to blue, orange, and yellow afterimages, respectively.

It appears possible that the subjects participating in the experiments that yielded positive results, namely, the experiments of Erickson and Erickson (1938), Rosenthal and Mele (1952), and Barber (1959), also had prior knowledge of the negative afterimage phenomenon. The subjects participating in these experiments almost always described the afterimage of hallucinated blue as yellow, of hallucinated green as red, and vice versa. Although introductory texts give the

[5] Many of these issues were discussed by Segal in the previous chapter. In many instances, the same articles were cited. However, Segal's conclusions are quite notably different from Barber's. Close reading of the relevant sections in the two papers will reveal that there is no real difference of opinion concerning the content of the papers cited, but rather in the relative emphases and the interpretation. Since the interpretations could not be reconciled without seriously violating the viewpoint of at least one of the two authors, the controversy is retained, and the reader can arrive at his own conclusions. (Editorial note.)

impression that blue produces a yellow afterimage, green a red afterimage, and vice versa, there are two reasons why these are misleading statements:

1. When individuals actually look at primary colors, they do *not* describe the negative afterimages in the simplified manner that is stated in introductory texts or in the manner of subjects giving a "correct" performance in the experiments of Erickson and Erickson, Rosenthal and Mele, and Barber. On the contrary, many subjects describe the afterimage of red as various shades of blue (not as green), many subjects describe the afterimage of green as pink, purplish pink, or violet (not as red), and many subjects describe the afterimage of yellow as violet or purple (not as blue) (Elsea, 1961).

2. Not only are there wide interindividual differences in the descriptions of the colors of afterimages, but as Downey (1901) observed, "even under the most unvarying conditions variations in the results obtained from any one individual will occur."

The above considerations suggest that, in the experiments of Erickson and Erickson, Rosenthal and Mele, and Barber, the subjects (college students) who reported red as the afterimage of hallucinated green, blue as the afterimage of hallucinated yellow, and vice versa, may have previously read about the negative afterimage phenomenon. As Sutcliffe (1960) has cogently noted, carefully controlled studies are needed to determine whether individuals who do not have prior knowledge of the afterimage phenomenon experience negative afterimages to vividly imagined or hallucinated colors. Further studies along these lines will have an important bearing in understanding the ramifications of processes labeled as "vivid imagining" or hallucinating.[6]

OPTICAL ILLUSIONS

To determine whether suggested hallucinations produce objective consequences which resemble those produced by actual visual stimulation, Underwood (1960) and Sarbin and Andersen (1963) used two optical illusions in which a series of lines distort a geometric figure. The subjects were shown the geometric figures *without* the distorting lines and were given suggestions to imagine vividly or to hallucinate the lines. If vivid imagining or hallucinating produces objective consequences similar to those produced by visual perception or visual stimulation, then the hallucination of the lines should produce an optical illusion, that is, should

---

[6]Several investigators have reported that some subjects with eidetic imagery perceive negative afterimages when they visualize colors (Kluver, 1928). The considerations mentioned above with respect to hallucinated colors also apply to the earlier studies on eidetic imagery. That is, it appears possible that the eidetic subjects had prior knowledge of the negative afterimage phenomenon, and it remains to be determined whether eidetic subjects who do not have such prior knowledge report negative afterimages when they visualize colors.

produce distortions in the appearance of the geometric figure. (Since the optical illusions were culled from obscure research reports, the investigators could be practically certain that the subjects were not previously acquainted with them.)

Underwood (1960) selected 6 subjects (from an original group of 195) as the most hypnotizable and as having the greatest ability to hallucinate. The 6 subjects were exposed to a hypnotic induction procedure and, when they were judged to be in "deep trance," were shown the geometric figures and given suggestions to hallucinate the lines superimposed upon them. Each of the 6 hypnotic subjects testified that he could clearly see the (suggested) lines. A control group, comprised of 6 unselected subjects, was asked to guess in what way the geometric figures would be distorted if the lines were superimposed. As compared to the control group, there was a nonsignificant tendency for the hypnotic subjects to report more distortions in the geometric figures. However, the distortions in the geometric figures produced by the hallucinated lines differed in several important respects from the distortions produced by the actual lines.

Sarbin and Andersen (1963) conducted a related study with 120 unselected college students. Under normal (nonhypnotic) conditions, the subjects were shown the same geometric figures that had been used by Underwood and were asked to imagine vividly that the lines were superimposed. Nine percent of the subjects reported some distortions in the geometric figures which tended to resemble those normally produced by the optical illusion but were not identical with them. Unfortunately, Sarbin and Andersen did not use a control group of subjects asked to try to figure out how the geometric figures would be distorted if the lines were superimposed.

In brief, the experiments of Underwood and of Sarbin and Andersen failed to demonstrate that hallucinating or vivid imagining produces effects which are similar to those produced by actual visual stimulation by an optical illusion figure. However, these experiments offer some tentative support for the hypothesis that hallucinating or vivid imagining may give rise to *some* objective effects. Further studies with the optical illusions which are designed to test the hypothesis should, of course, compare a group of hallucinating subjects with a group told simply to try to figure out the effect.

NYSTAGMUS

When an individual gazes steadily at a rotating kymograph drum which is painted with vertical black and white stripes, he manifests nystagmus, that is, his eyes move rhythmically from side to side, quickly to one side and then slowly to the other. Brady and Levitt (1966) reasoned that if visual hallucinations induced in hypnotic subjects produce objective effects similar to those produced by visual stimulation, then the hypnotic subjects should show nystagmus when they hallucinate the rotating black and white drum. To test this hypothesis, 9 hypnotic subjects were carefully selected from an original group of 48 individuals as meeting criteria for vivid visual hallucinations. During the experiment, eye movements were monitored electrically on a polygraph. The selected subjects first watched the black and white stripes rotating on the drum. The drum was removed and, after a hypnotic induction procedure was administered, suggestions were given to induce a hallucination of the rotating drum. When hallucinating the rotating drum, 1 of the 9 hypnotic subjects showed nystagmus 70% of the time, 3 showed nystagmus about 10% of the time, and the remaining 5 subjects did not manifest nystagmus.

Hahn and Barber (1966) conducted a similar experiment but they did not use hypnotic induction procedures. The technique for measuring nystagmus was the same as that used by Brady and Levitt (1966). Nine unselected subjects were tested individually under normal (nonhypnotic) conditions. Each subject first watched the black and white stripes rotating on the drum. After the drum was removed each subject was instructed to imagine vividly and to visualize the rotating black and white drum. When vividly imagining the rotating drum, 1 of the 9 subjects showed clear-cut nystagmus. Rhythmical side-to-side movements of the eyes (quickly to one side and then slowly to the other) were present more than 90% of the time when the subject was vividly imagining the rotating drum regardless of whether her eyes were open or closed. Of the remaining 8 subjects, 3 showed nystagmus at least 35% of the time when they were imagining the rotating drum and the remaining 5 did not show nystagmus.

In both the Brady and Levitt and the Hahn and Barber experiments, the subjects failed to manifest nystagmus when they were asked to try to produce it voluntarily. However, Reich (1970) recently presented data indicating that some subjects are able to produce nystagmus "through conscious, voluntary efforts while awake."

In brief, the studies of Brady and Levitt (1966) and of Hahn and Barber (1966) appeared to indicate that when vividly imagining or hallucinating a black and white rotating drum some individuals show eye movements (nystagmus) which resemble those found when they actually look at the rotating drum. However, since a recent study (Reich, 1970) indicates that some subjects can produce nystagmus voluntarily, extreme caution is needed in interpreting these results. Further studies are needed before we can unequivocally reject or accept the hypothesis that vivid imagining or hallucinating per se gives rise to an objective effect (nystagmus) which resembles that produced by actual visual stimulation.

SUMMARY AND CONCLUSIONS

Although LSD produces a wide variety of effects, including alterations in body-image, in tactile sensitivity, and in perception of time, I have focused in this paper on the effect of LSD on visual perception. When an individual closes his eyes after he has taken a moderate dose of LSD, he typically perceives vividly colored forms. Also, when his eyes are open, he reports a change in his perception of colors and in the size and shape of objects, persons, and his own body. Speaking more generally, LSD affects the constancies of perception and tends to produce distortions, illusions, vivid imagery, and hallucinations.

The subject's attitudes, expectancies, and personality characteristics may affect the contents of the LSD visual phenomena. As compared to individuals with ordinary imagery, individuals with strong imagery (who normally project their visual images in front of their eyes) report more intense visual phenomena with LSD. Also, the characteristics of the visual phenomena may be affected to some extent by explicit or implicit suggestions. However, these kinds of variables, suggestions, expectancies, personality characteristics, etc., have been overemphasized in previous discussions of this topic. Although the characteristics of the subject and suggestions imbedded in the situation may play a role, they are *not* the most important factors either in eliciting the LSD visual phenomena or in determining their contents or intensity. What needs to be emphasized now is that the visual phenomena associated with LSD are closely correlated with the *dose* of the drug. The number and intensity of the visual phenomena are strongly associated with the dose of LSD and weakly associated with the subject's expectancies and with suggestions that are present in the situation.[7]

It appears that LSD gives rise to changes in visual perception by producing physiological changes in the visual system. Some of the visual phenomena associated with LSD appear to be closely related to alterations produced by this drug on structures within the eyeball (the pupil, the lens, the intraocular fluid, and the retina). This includes the blurring of vision, difficulties in focusing, and the rainbow-effect. The distortions in spatial perception and the alterations in the constancies of perception which are associated with LSD may be due to the partial paralysis of the ciliary muscle (and the concomitant deficiency in the accommodating power of the lens). The vivid patterns that are perceived with eyes closed may be related both to the increased intraocular pressure which is produced by LSD and also to a direct effect of this drug on the retina.

Some, but not all, of the visual phenomena associated with LSD appear to be due to a physiological effect of this drug on structures within the eyeball. However, to understand all of the LSD visual phenomena we need to delineate more precisely the effects of LSD on the entire visual system. The data at present suggest that LSD does not simply affect the functioning of structures within the eyeball; it appears that LSD also affects the lateral geniculates and the occipital cortex and, more generally, exerts an effect on the functioning of the total visual system.

[7] Although the *dose* of LSD accounts for most of the variance with respect to the *visual phenomena,* suggestions, expectancies, attitudes, personality characteristics and other non-drug variables are the critical factors in determining the subject's moods, emotions, and cognitions in the drug situation (Barber, 1970).

It has been stated that the vivid imagery or hallucinations that are produced by LSD can also be produced by suggestions given under hypnosis. However, it seems that the hypnotic or suggested phenomena differ in several important respects from the LSD phenomena.

When unselected subjects (college students or nursing students) are exposed to a hypnotic induction procedure and are given suggestions to see an object that is not actually present, more than half report that they clearly see the object. However, when the subjects are told at the beginning of the experiment and several times during the experiment that honest reports are wanted, less than 20% of the hypnotic subjects report that they clearly see the suggested object. Also, when an honest report is demanded once at the end of the experiment, about 20% of unselected subjects who have *not* been exposed to a hypnotic induction procedure (controls) state that they clearly see the suggested object.

It is by no means clear, at the present time, what these subjects (around 20% in a hypnotic group and also in a control group) mean when they report that they clearly see a suggested object. Unfortunately, no empirical studies have as yet ascertained whether subjects mean that they see the suggested object in the same way they see an actual object or in the same way they see a negative or positive afterimage, or whether they simply mean that they see it clearly in their mind's eye.

Regardless of whether or not some subjects see a suggested object out there and others see it in their mind's eye, it has not as yet been shown that these suggested hallucinations give rise to objective effects which are independent of the subjects' verbal reports. There is no clear evidence that suggested hallucinations give rise to pupillary dilations or contractions, or to negative afterimages. Also, a suggested hallucination of an optical illusion does not have the same effects as an actual illusion. And, even though vivid imagery of revolving stripes may produce objective nystagmus, this is not a conclusive demonstration, as nystagmus can be produced voluntarily.

In brief, it appears that subjects who have taken LSD experience alterations in visual perception which are based on physiological changes that have occurred throughout the visual system. The effects of suggestions to hallucinate (given under either hypnotic or nonhypnotic conditions) appear to differ qualitatively from the visual effects of LSD. There is no evidence that suggestions to hallucinate produce physiological changes in the visual system which affect visual perception. In fact, the hypothesis that needs to be tested in further research is that suggestions to hallucinate simply induce the subject to imagine or to image to the best of his ability.

REFERENCES

Abramson, H. A. Lysergic acid diethylamide (LSD-25): XXX. The questionnaire technique with notes on its use. *Journal of Psychology,* 1960, **49,** 57-65.

Abramson, H. A., Kornetsky, C., Jarvik, M. E., Kaufman, M. R., & Ferguson, M. W. Lysergic acid diethylamide (LSD-25): XI. Content analysis of clinical reactions. *Journal of Psychology*, 1955, **40**, 53-60.

Adler, F. H. *Textbook of ophthalmology*. (7th ed.) Philadelphia: W. B. Saunders, 1962.

Anderson, E. W., & Rawnsley, K. Clinical studies of lysergic acid diethylamide. *Monatsschrift für Psychiatrie und Neurologie*, 1954, **128**, 38-55.

Apter, J. T., & Pfeiffer, C. C. The effects of the hallucinogenic drugs LSD-25 and mescaline on the electroretinogram. *Annals of the New York Academy Sciences*, 1957, **66** (Art. 3) 508-514.

Balestrieri, A., & Fontanari, D. Acquired and crossed tolerance to mescaline, LSD-25, and BOL-148. *Archives of General Psychiatry*, 1959, **1**, 279-282.

Barber, T. X. The after-images of "imagined" and "hallucinated" colors. *Journal of Abnormal and Social Psychology*, 1959, **59**, 136-139.

Barber, T. X. Experimental controls and the phenomena of "hypnosis": A critique of hypnotic research methodology. *Journal of Nervous and Mental Diseases*, 1962, **134**, 493-505.

Barber, T. X. Hypnotically hallucinated colors and their negative after-images. *American Journal of Psychology*, 1964, **77**, 313-318.

Barber, T. X. "Hypnotic" phenomena: A critique of experimental methods. In J. E. Gordon (Ed.) *Handbook of clinical and experimental hypnosis*. New York: Macmillan, 1967.

Barber, T. X. *Hypnosis: A scientific approach*. New York: Van Nostrand Reinhold, 1969. (a)

Barber, T. X. "Hypnosis," suggestions, and auditory-visual "hallucinations": A critical analysis. Paper presented at Eastern Psychiatric Research Association, New York, November 14, 1969. (b)

Barber, T. X. *LSD, marihuana, yoga, and hypnosis*. Chicago: Aldine, 1970.

Barber, T. X., & Calverley, D. S. An experimental study of "hypnotic" (auditory and visual) hallucinations. *Journal of Abnormal and Social Psychology*, 1964, **68**, 13-20.

Barber, T. X. & Silver, M. J. Fact, fiction, and the experimenter bias effect. *Psychological Bulletin*, 1968, **70**, No. 6, Part 2 (Monograph Supplement), 1-29. (a)

Barber, T. X., & Silver, M. J. Pitfalls in data analysis and interpretation: A reply to Rosenthal. *Psychological Bulletin*, 1968, **70**, No. 6, Part 2 (Monograph Supplement), 48-62. (b)

Barber, T. X., Spanos, N., & Merritt, J. The effect of strong demands for honesty on the suggested ("hypnotic") hallucination. Harding, Mass.: Medfield Foundation, 1970.

Bercel, N. A., Travis, L. E., Olinger, L. B., & Dreikurs, E. Model psychoses induced by LSD-25 in normals: I. Psychophysiological investigations with special reference to the mechanism of the paranoid reaction. *Archives of Neurology and Psychiatry*, 1956, **75**, 588-611.

Bertino, J. R., Klee, G. D., Collier, D., & Weintraub, W. Clinical studies with dibenzyline and lysergic acid diethylamide. *Journal of Clinical and Experimental Psychopathology*, 1960, **21**, 293-299.

Bowers, K. S. The effects of demands for honesty on reports of visual and auditory hallucinations. *International Journal of Clinical and Experimental Hypnosis*, 1967, **15**, 31-36.

Brady, J. P., & Levitt, E. E. Hypnotically induced visual hallucinations. *Psychosomatic Medicine*, 1966, **28**, 351-363.

Brown, B. B. Subjective and EEG responses to LSD in visualizer and nonvisualizer subjects. *EEG Clinical Neurophysiology*, 1968, **25**, 372-379.

Burian, H. M., Fleming, W. J., & Featherstone, R. M. Electroretinographic effects of LSD-25, Brom-LSD, and LSM (lysergic acid morpholide). *Federation Proceedings*, 1958, **17**, 355.

Cohen, S. *The beyond within: The LSD story*. (2nd ed.) New York: Atheneum, 1967.

Cohen, S. A quarter century of research with LSD. In J. T. Ungerleider (Ed.), *The problem and prospects of LSD*. Springfield, Ill.: C. C. Thomas, 1968.

Ditman, K. S., Moss, T., Forgy, E. W., Zunin, L. M., Lynch, R. D., & Funk, W. A. Dimensions of the LSD, methylphenidate, and chlordiazepoxide experiences. *Psychopharmacologia,* 1969, **14,** 1-11.

Dobie, S. Operant conditioning of verbal and hallucinatory responses with nonverbal reinforcement. Paper presented at Midwestern Psychological Association, Chicago, May, 1959.

Dorcus, R. M. Modification by suggestion of some vestibular and visual responses. *American Journal of Psychology,* 1937, **49,** 82-87.

Downey, J. E. An experiment on getting an after-image from a mental image. *Psychological Review,* 1901, 8, 42- 55.

Edwards, A. E., & Cohen, S. Visual illusion, tactile sensibility and reaction time under LSD-25. *Psychopharmacologia,* 1961, **2,** 297-303.

Edwards, A. E., & Cohen, S. Interaction of LSD and quantity of encoded visual data upon size estimation. *Journal of Psychopharmacology,* 1966, **1,** 96-100.

Elsea, O. C., Jr. A study of the effect of hypnotic suggestion on color perception. Unpublished doctoral dissertation, University of Oklahoma, 1961.

Erickson, M. H., & Erickson, E. M. The hypnotic induction of hallucinatory color vision followed by pseudo negative after images. *Journal of Experimental Psychology,* 1938, **22,** 581-588.

Estabrooks, G. H. *Hypnotism.* New York: E. P. Dutton, 1943.

Farnsworth, N. R. Hallucinogenic plants. *Science,* 1968, **162,** 1086-1092.

Fiddleman, P. B. The prediction of behavior under lysergic acid diethylamide (LSD). Unpublished doctoral dissertation, University of North Carolina, 1961.

Fisher, S. Problems of interpretation and controls in hypnotic research. In G. H. Estabrooks (Ed.) *Hypnosis: Current problems.* New York: Harper & Row, 1962.

Fogel, S., & Hoffer, A. The use of hypnosis to interrupt and to reproduce an LSD-25 experience. *Journal of Clinical and Experimental Psychopathology,* 1962, **23,** 11-16.

Goldiamond, I., & Malpass, L. F. Locus of hypnotically induced changes in color vision responses. *Journal of the Optical Society of America,* 1961, **51,** 1117-1121.

Hahn, K. W., Jr., & Barber, T. X. Hallucinations with and without hypnotic induction: An extension of the Brady and Levitt study. Harding, Mass.: Medfield Foundation, 1966.

Hartman, A. M., & Hollister, L. E. Effect of mescaline, lysergic acid diethylamide and psilocybin on color perception. *Psychopharmacologia,* 1963, **4,** 441-451.

Heaton, J. M. *The eye: Phenomenology and psychology of function and disorder.* Philadelphia: J. B. Lippincott, 1968.

Hibler, F. W. An experimental study of positive visual hallucinations in hypnosis. Unpublished doctoral dissertation, Ohio State University, 1935.

Hibler, F. W. An experimental investigation of negative after-images of hallucinated colors in hypnosis. *Journal of Experimental Psychology,* 1940, **27,** 45-57.

Hilgard, E. R. *Hypnotic susceptibility.* New York: Harcourt, Brace & World, 1965.

Hoffer, A., & Osmond, H. *The hallucinogens.* New York: Academic Press, 1967.

Holliday, A. R., & Sigurdson, T. The effects of lysergic acid diethylamide II: Intraocular pressure. *Proceedings of the Western Pharmacological Society,* 1965, **8,** 51-54.

Hollister, L. E. *Chemical psychoses: LSD and related drugs.* Springfield, Ill.: C. C. Thomas, 1968.

Hollister, L. E., & Hartman, A. M. Mescaline, lysergic acid diethylamide and psilocybin: Comparison of clinical syndromes, effects on color perception, and biochemical measures. *Comprehensive Psychiatry,* 1962, **3,** 235-241.

Hollister, L. E., Macnicol, M. F., & Gillespie, H. K. An hallucinogenic amphetamine analog (DOM) in man. *Psychopharmacologia,* 1969, **14,** 62-73.

Huxley, A. *The doors of perception.* New York: Harper, 1954.

Isbell, H. Comparison of the reactions induced by psilocybin and LSD-25 in man. *Psychopharmacologia,* 1959, **1,** 29-38.

Isbell, H. *Studies on tetrahydrocannabinol. I. Method of assay in human subjects and results with crude extracts, purified tetrahydrocannabinols and synthetic compounds.* Lexington, Kentucky: University of Kentucky Medical Center, 1967.

Isbell, H., Belleville, R. E., Fraser, H. F., Wikler, A., & Logan, C. R. Studies on lysergic acid diethylamide (LSD-25): I. Effects in former morphine addicts and development of tolerance during chronic intoxication. *Archives of Neurology and Psychiatry,* 1956, **76,** 468-478.

Isbell, H., Gorodetzsky, C. W. Jasinski, D., Claussen, U., Spulak, F. V., & Korte, F. Effects of (−)-Δ^9trans-tetrahydrocannabinol in man. *Psychopharmacologia,* 1967, **11,** 184-188.

Isbell, H., Wolbach, A. B., Wikler, A., & Miner, E. J. Cross-tolerance between LSD and psilocybin. *Psychopharmacologia,* 1961, **2,** 147-151.

Jacobson, J. H., & Gestring, G. F. Spontaneous retinal electrical potentials. *Archives of Ophthalmology,* 1959, **62,** 599-603.

Johnson, F. G. LSD in the treatment of alcoholism. Paper presented at American Psychiatric Association, Boston, June, 1968.

Keeler, M. H. The effects of psilocybin on a test of after-image perception. *Psychopharmacologia,* 1965, **8,** 131-139.

Kieffer, S. N., & Moritz, T. B. Psychedelic drugs. *Pennsylvania Medicine,* 1968, **71,** 57-67.

Klee, G. D., Bertino, J., Weintraub, W., & Callaway, E. The influence of varying dosage on the effects of lysergic acid diethylamide (LSD-25) in humans. *Journal of Nervous and Mental Disease,* 1961, **132,** 404-409.

Kluver, H. Studies on the eidetic type and on eidetic imagery. *Psychological Bulletin,* 1928, **25,** 69-104.

Kluver, H. *Mescal and mechanisms of hallucination.* Chicago: University of Chicago Press, 1966.

Knoll, M., & Kugler, J. Subjective light-pattern spectroscopy in the electroencephalographic frequency range. *Nature,* 1959, **184,** 1823.

Knoll, M., Kugler, J., Hofer, O., & Lawder, S. D. Effects of chemical stimulation of electrically induced phosphenes on their bandwidth, shape, number and intensity. *Confinia Neurologica,* 1963, **23,** 201-226.

Krill, A. E., Alpert, H. J., & Ostfeld, A. M. Effects of a hallucinogenic agent in totally blind subjects. *Archives of Ophthalmology,* 1963, **69,** 180-185.

Krill, A. E., Wieland, A. M., & Ostfeld, A. M. The effects of two hallucinogenic agents on human retinal function. *Archives of Ophthalmology,* 1960, **64,** 724-733.

Ladd-Franklin, C. Visible radiation from excited nerve fiber: The reddish blue arcs and the reddish blue glow of the retina. *Science,* 1927, **66,** 239-241.

Levis, D. J., & Mehlman, B. Suggestion and mescaline sulphate. *Journal of Neuropsychiatry,* 1964, **5,** 197-200.

Liebert, R. S., Wapner, S., & Werner, H. Studies in the effects of lysergic acid diethylamide (LSD-25). Visual perception of verticality in schizophrenic and normal adults. *Archives of Neurology and Psychiatry,* 1957, **77,** 193-201.

Lundholm, H. A hormic theory of hallucinations. *British Journal of Medical Psychology,* 1932, **11,** 269-282.

Marshall, C. R. An enquiry into the causes of mescal vision. *Journal of Neuropathology and Psychopathology,* 1937, **17,** 289-304.

Masters, R. E. L., & Houston, J. *The varieties of psychedelic experience.* New York: Holt, 1966.

Murphy, D. B., & Meyers, T. I. Occurrence, measurement, and experimental manipulation of visual "hallucinations." *Perceptual and Motor Skills,* 1962, **15,** 47-54.

Naruse, G. Hypnosis as a state of meditative concentration and its relationship to the perceptual process. In M. V. Kline (Ed.), *The nature of hypnosis.* New York: Institute for Research in Hypnosis, 1962.

Pahnke, W. N., & Richards, W. A. Implications of LSD and experimental mysticism. *Journal of Religion and Health,* 1966, **5,** 175-208.

Payne, J. W. LSD-25 and accommodative convergence ratios. *Archives of Ophthalmology,* 1965, **74,** 81-85.

Penfield, W. *The excitable cortex in conscious man.* Springfield, Ill.: C. C. Thomas, 1958.

Purpura, D. P. Neurophysiological actions of LSD. In R. C. Debold and R. C. Leaf (Eds.) *LSD, man and society.* Middletown, Conn.: Wesleyan University Press, 1967.

Reich, L. H. Optokinetic nystagmus during hypnotic hallucinations. Paper presented at Eastern Psychological Association, Atlantic City, April 4, 1970.

Rodin, E., & Luby, E. Effects of LSD-25 on the EEG and photic evoked responses. *Archives of General Psychiatry,* 1966, **14,** 435-441.

Rosenberg, D. E., Isbell, H., Miner, E. J., & Logan, C. R. The effects of *N,N*-dimethyltryptamine in human subjects tolerant to lysergic acid diethylamide. *Psychopharmacologia,* 1964, **5,** 217-227.

Rosenthal, B. G., & Mele, H. The validity of hypnotically induced color hallucinations. *Journal of Abnormal and Social Psychology,* 1952, **47,** 700-704.

Rosenthal, R. Experimenter expectancy and the reassuring nature of the null hypothesis decision procedure. *Psychological Bulletin,* 1968, **70,** No. 6, Part 2 (Monograph Supplement), 30-47.

Sarbin, T. R., & Andersen, M. L. Base-rate expectancies and perceptual alterations in hypnosis. *British Journal of Clinical Psychology,* 1963, **2,** 112-121.

Schultes, R. E. Hallucinogens of plant origin. *Science,* 1969, **163,** 245-254.

Short, W. B., Jr. The effects of drugs on the electroretinogram of the cat. *Journal of Pharmacology and Experimental Therapeutics,* 1958, **122,** 68A.

Shryne, J. E., Jr., & Brown, B. B. Effect of LSD on responses to colored photic stimuli as related to visual imagery ability in man. *Proceedings of the Western Pharmacological Society,* 1965, **8,** 42-46.

Sidis, B. Are there hypnotic hallucinations? *Psychological Review,* 1906, **13,** 239-257.

Snyder, S. H., Faillace, L., & Hollister, L. 2,5-Dimethoxy-4-methylamphetamine (STP): A new hallucinogenic drug. *Science,* 1967, **158,** 669-670.

Snyder, S. H., Faillace, L. A., & Weingartner, H. DOM (STP) a new hallucinogenic drug, and DOET: Effects in normal subjects. *American Journal of Psychiatry,* 1968, **125,** 357-364.

Snyder, S. H., & Reivich, M. Regional localization of lysergic acid diethylamide in monkey brain. *Nature,* 1966, **209,** 1093-1095.

Spanos, N. P., & Barber, T. X. "Hypnotic" experiences as inferred from subjective reports: Auditory and visual hallucinations. *Journal of Experimental Research in Personality,* 1968, **3,** 136-150.

Sutcliffe, J. P. "Credulous" and "sceptical" views of hypnotic phenomena: A review of certain evidence and methodology. *International Journal of Clinical and Experimental Hypnosis,* 1960, **8,** 73-101.

Szara, S., Rockland, L. H., Rosenthal, D., & Handlon, J. H. Psychological effects and metabolism of *N,N*-diethyltryptamine in man. *Archives of General Psychiatry,* 1966, **15,** 320-329.

Underwood, H. W. The validity of hypnotically induced visual hallucinations. *Journal of Abnormal and Social Psychology,* 1960, **61,** 39-46.

Unger, S. M. Mescaline, LSD, psilocybin, and personality change. *Psychiatry,* 1963, **26,** 111-125.

Weckowicz, T. E. The effect of lysergic acid diethylamide (LSD) on size constancy. *Canadian Psychiatric Association Journal,* 1959, **4,** 255-259.

Weinberger, L. M., & Grant, F. C. Visual hallucinations and their neuro-optical correlates. *Ophthalmologic Reviews,* 1940, **23,** 166-199.

Weitzenhoffer, A. M. *Hypnotism: An objective study in suggestibility.* New York: Wiley, 1953.

White, H. E., & Levatin, P. "Floaters" in the eyes. *Scientific American,* 1962, **206,** No. 6, 119-127.

Wolbach, A. B., Miner, E. J., & Isbell, H. Comparison of psilocin with psilocybin, mescaline, and LSD-25 *Psychopharmacologia,* 1962, **3,** 219-223.

AUTHOR INDEX

SUBJECT INDEX